EXPLORING THE REGENT'S CANAL

To Nicholas

Bust outside All Souls Church, Langham Place, London.

EXPLORING

THE

REGENT'S CANAL

Michael Essex-Lopresti

K.A.F. BREWIN BOOKS
STUDLEY 1987

Published by
K.A.F. Brewin Books, Studley, Warwickshire
May 1987
New Edition March 1989

By the same author:
EXPLORING THE NEW RIVER

ISBN 0 947731 40 7

Typeset in Press Roman and
made and printed in Great Britain
by Supaprint (Redditch) Ltd., Redditch, Worcs.

To Lorna, my wife, and to Jane and Sally,
who have heard it all so often

CONTENTS

INTRODUCTION

My wife and I bought a boat on the canals some fifteen years ago and that is when our exploration of the inland waterways in Britain began. Once our interest had been aroused we began attending courses and guided walks to learn more about the system. A guided walk along the Regent's Canal in London was, I was told by the organiser, to be the last due to lack of support. This seemed a pity so I wrote to the Inland Waterways Association suggesting that it was the appropriate body to arrange such walks; after some deliberation I was informed that my suggestion had been accepted by the London Branch — and that I was nominated for the task.

So it was that I began to study the Regent's Canal in detail — a study which has continued ever since — and the regular monthly walks, started in 1977, recently achieved their first decade. During this time I have maintained a close liaison with a variety of authorities which has given me the opportunity of obtaining a wealth of information on past and present features of the canal. I began lecturing regularly to a wide range of audiences and a number of radio and television interviews on the Regent's Canal brought me new invitations to lead groups on walks along it, and to give talks to those planning a cruise. In 1985 I was invited to provide a commentary on the Limehouse Cruise arranged by the London Waterbus Company and this I do regularly.

With the publication of my book "Exploring the New River" I was encouraged to consider the preparation of a similar book on the Regent's Canal, using the same format. The book is in three main sections. First is a brief history which aims to provide the reader with sufficient detail for him or her to appreciate the relevance of structures to be seen on the canal; the books listed in the bibliography give far more detail on the preparation, construction and fortunes of the canal and I can recommend them for further reading. I so enjoy reading contemporary descriptions of the canal and its surrounding neighbourhood that I have reproduced, in the second part of the book, selected passages to provide a flavour of the style of the period. The third section contains detailed descriptions of features to be seen by anybody walking along the towing path and over Maida Hill and Islington tunnels, with supplementary information to add to the interest.

Throughout the book are passages quoted from a variety of sources; as far as possible I consulted the original document for each quotation and transcribed it as accurately as possible, copying the spelling, punctuation and capital or lower case initial letters. Several of the books have been re-printed by other publishers — for instance Dicken's Dictionary of London 1877 (Howard Baker 1972), John Hassell's Tour of the Grand Junction Canal 1819 (Cranfield & Bonfiel 1968) and Frederick William's The Midland Railway 1878 (Augustus Kelley 1960) — and in these changes in the text, punctuation and spelling have been introduced; St Pancrass became St Pancras, for instance (see page 22). In the early 19th century it was common in newspapers and magazines to print 'road' and 'street', following names, without capitals — sometimes with hyphens such as City-road and Regent's-park-road. The only variation from the original I have introduced is £ before numerals instead of 1 after them; I take the view that £50,000 is easier to read than 50,0001, which was common until the mid-19th century.

Michael Essex-Lopresti
January, 1987

ACKNOWLEDGEMENTS

The preparation of a book on the Regent's Canal requires a lot of reading of historical documents and of books written by others; the source material is limited so it is inevitable that much of the information included has already appeared in print and I express my gratitude to the authors of the books listed in the bibliography for leading me to material of which I might otherwise have been unaware.

My special thanks go to Gordon Dodd and Frank Bamping who read my drafts, making many helpful suggestions and corrections. The staff in the Local History Departments of the London Boroughs of Camden, Hackney, Islington, Tower Hamlets and the City of Westminster, and in the London Records Office and History Library have produced a wealth of maps and references for me and I have had valuable help from the British Waterways Board and the Inland Waterways Association and from many people who remember the canal as it used to be.

Most of the photographs were taken by me; the engravings were obtained as follows: Burton Warehouse 1870 from the Heal Collection in Camden Local History Library, Islington Tunnel 1819 from Islington Library, City Road Locks 1835 from Tower Hamlets Local History Collection, and Councillor Agar's House 1830 and St Pancras Station 1877 were taken from Walford's Old and New London. City Road Basin is reproduced from an oil painting I did in 1973 and Legging through a Tunnel is a sketch I did, based on an original in the London Borough of Camden Local History Department.

I am grateful to Brian Hague who helped me with the research at the start of the Guided Walks along the Regent's Canal, and to IWA members Len House, Arthur Gardner, John Hebbert and Maurice Plant who joined us as guides during the past decade, generously giving their time each month throughout the year. My wife has walked and cruised the canal with me for many years.

A BRIEF HISTORY OF THE REGENT'S CANAL

1.   Canals in Britain

Britain's first canals, like its roads, were built by the Romans during the first and second centuries.   The earliest are thought to be in the Lincolnshire area, near the junction of Fosse Way with Ermine Street, and it is believed that they started as drainage channels which were subsequently made navigable.   This is certainly true of Fosse Dyke, an eleven mile lock-free canal from the River Witham at Lincoln to Torksey on the River Trent which is navigable to this day.   Built in AD 120 it was later used by the Normans to carry stone to build Lincoln Cathedral. (1).   The Car Dyke, dug by the Romans from Lincoln to Peterborough and then into Cambridge-shire, was thought to be a navigable canal (2), a view suggested by the fact that excavation has shown it to have been some fifty feet across the top and thirty feet wide at the bottom, with a depth of eight feet.   Much of it is still to be seen as a wet ditch.   More recent work has shown that its course was not continuous and that its levels confirm its use as a drainage channel rather than a navigation. (3 & 4)

In medieval times, rivers were deepened and widened to make them navigable. Weirs were built to increase their depth and boats moved between the changes in level by means of 'flash locks', they were carried downstream over the 'lock' by the current or pulled up against the flow.   The first river to be improved for commercial use, by Act of Parliament, was the River Lee from Hertford to the Thames east of London, the Acts being dated 1424 and 1430, in the reign of Henry VI (5).   In Exeter the river between the city and the sea was blocked by a weir which obstructed shipping so the Exeter Canal was dug in 1566 alongside the estuary up to the docks.   This canal introduced to Britain locks of the modern type, consisting of a chamber, with gates at each end, large enough to contain a boat.   The locks on the Exeter Canal had vertically rising gates (6a), whereas the first lock with mitre gates – as we know them today – was built on the River Lee at Waltham Abbey following the 1571 Act.   This Act, in the reign of Queen Elizabeth I, required the straightening of the river by new cuts (5).

Most of the major canals in Britain were opened during the reign of one monarch – George III, 1760 – 1820.   The first entirely commercial canal built independent of a natural watercourse was the Bridgewater Canal from the Duke of Bridgewater's coal mines at Worsley into Manchester, with a branch to Liverpool.   The engineer on this canal was James Brindley who became enthusiastic about a grand network of canals linking the industrial midlands with the major ports at Hull, Liverpool, Bristol and London.   His proposal for the first of these between Hull and Liverpool was strongly supported by the potter, Josiah Wedgwood, who recognised the value of water trans-port for conveying his delicate pottery on a canal passing his factory; the Trent and Mersey Canal received Royal Assent in 1766 and construction began from Shardlow on the River Trent to Preston Brook where it would join the proposed extension of the Bridgewater Canal to Liverpool.   Brindley built the Birmingham Canal in 1768– 1772 and joined it to the Staffordshire and Worcester Canal down the Wolverhampton flight of twenty locks.   This Canal, linking the Trent and Mersey Canal to the River Severn at Stourport, was opened in 1772, the year he died.   Nevertheless his grand scheme was continued and the Oxford Canal from the Trent and Mersey (via the Coventry Canal) to the Thames at Oxford was completed in 1790.   The ports of Bristol and London were thereby incorporated into the network.

These were all narrow canals, with locks and bridge-holes for narrow boats not wider than seven feet, and they were contour canals which followed the lie of the land to avoid the need for too many changes of level requiring locks to be built. From 1800, however, several broad canals were opened — notably the Grand Junction Canal (1801) from Birmingham to the Thames at Brentford with an arm to Paddington in west London, the Kennet and Avon Canal (1810) from the Thames at Reading to Bath, the Leeds and Liverpool Canal (1816) over the Pennines and the Regent's Canal (1820) from Paddington, by way of the City, to the Thames at Limehouse. These broad canals would accept two narrow boats alongside each other in the locks, and it was hoped that the introduction of broad-beamed barges would ensure the future of the canals. These canals were dug straighter than the narrow canals, with aqueducts over valleys and tunnels through hills.

2.   London in the Canal Age

The need to establish and improve on the transport of merchandise to London was the source of much competition during the eighteenth and nineteenth centuries. Initially goods were moved mainly on trunk roads, but in the east boats on the River Lee Navigation were carrying grain, corn and malt from Hertfordshire to the City. Then in 1790 the Oxford Canal opened up the route from Birmingham and the Midlands to London by way of the Thames from Oxford and in 1801 the Grand Junction Canal was opened to Paddington in west London, cutting some sixty miles off the Birmingham Journey (1). It terminated at Paddington because that was near one end of the New Road, a highway which formed the northern boundary of London, where goods could be transferred to carts for haulage by horses to Islington and the City. The New Road was built in the mid eighteenth century and it was intended as "the boundary line for limiting the 'ruinous rage for building' on the north side of the town." (7a).

"The New Road, connecting the corner of Lisson Grove with the village of Islington, was formed in 1757, not without great opposition from the Duke of Bedford, who succeeded in obtaining the insertion of a clause in the Act forbidding any building being erected within fifty feet of either side of the roadway." (7b). Horace Walpole, in a letter to General Conway in March, 1756, commented "A new road through Paddington (to the City) has been projected, to avoid the stones. The Duke of Bedford, who is never in town in the summer, objects to the dust it will make behind Bedford House, and to some buildings proposed (no doubt, in the rear of his gardens), though if he were in town he is too short-sighted to see the prospect." (7c). The New Road played a significant role in London's transport needs. It linked several major routes from the west and north and it crossed the great north road — Maiden Lane (now York Way) — at Battle Bridge where in 1830 a great statue of George VI was mounted on a massive plinth and the name of the area was changed to Kings Cross (see page 52). Traffic could use it to by-pass the City, and several markets, including the Cumberland Market — later to be served by the proposed canal — were built close to it.

To the north of the New Road lay Marylebone Park and Marylebone Farm. Once part of Henry VIII's hunting forest, the land had been leased by the Duke of Portland in 1789 and a Commission was set up in 1796 to inquire into the bad management and neglect of the Crown property (8). John Fordyce, who was appointed Surveyor-General of His Majesty's Land Revenue, suggested that the park should be developed and that London should be extended into it. Nothing happened until 1810 when it was realised that the Duke of Portland's lease was about to expire. The architects to the Department of Land Revenue — Thomas Leverton and Thomas Nash and his assistant James Morgan — were each asked to prepare designs for the development of the Marylebone Estate. That prepared by Nash and Morgan was accepted and it is said to have so delighted the Prince of Wales, lately appointed as Prince Regent, that he allowed Nash to call it Regent's Park. James Elmes, the architect, commented that Nash had "metamorphosed Mary-le-bone Park Farm and its cowsheds into a rural city of almost eastern magnificence" (8). By 1840 London was extending beyond the New Road in several places, notably the slums of Somers Town and then Agar Town (see page 30).

Soon after the Grand Junction Canal had opened to Paddington Basin on 10 July, 1801, it was natural that somebody would suggest a canal, running parallel with the New Road between Paddington and the City, to avoid the transhipment of goods between barge and cart. As this was the northern limit of London, the canal could run through the open country just north of the road. When the railways reached London, all the railway companies wanted their main line termini on the New Road, and as by then the canal had been cut, the railways would have to cross the water to reach the road. This caused them problems (see page 15). Today the line of the New Road is seen in Marylebone, Euston and Pentonville Roads; all the railways from the north and west have their termini on it — Paddington, Marylebone, Euston, St. Pancras and Kings Cross — and no line extended beyond it southwards. Incidentally the first underground railway, the Metropolitan Line built to alleviate the traffic in North London, was built under the New Road from Paddington to Farringdon in 1863, and therefore serves all the north London Main Line termini.

It is clear that the area north of Marylebone Road and Euston Road is now part of the London connurbation and it is likely that the advent of the canal had some influence on it; factories and workshops need good transport for their supplies — coal, timber, stone etc. — and for the carriage of their products, and they would need wharfs alongside the canal. But the first incursion beyond the limit of London began as the canal was being built, with the construction of residential properties by John Nash in Regent's Park.

The "New Road" today — Marylebone Road.

3

3.   Proposals for a London Canal

Within a year of the opening of the Paddington Canal – as the Arm of the Grand Junction Canal was sometimes called – Thomas Homer was considering the possibility of a London Canal, running parallel to the New Road to Islington, and extending it to the Thames at Limehouse where a ship dock would be built.   The canal engineer, John Rennie, reported favourably on the project but no progress was made until in 1811 Homer discovered that John Nash had been appointed to develop the Marylebone Park Estate – later Regent's Park.   Homer approached Nash inviting him to undertake responsibility for the canal and Nash, we are told, was delighted at the prospect of boats sailing through the middle of his park (9) and he accepted.   Nash and his assistant, James Morgan, were joined by an engineer, James Tate, to examine Homer's proposed route and, with minor adjustments agreed it.   Nash was now fully involved in the Marylebone Park scheme and though originally he had intended that the canal should run through the centre of the Park, perhaps it was not realised at the time that the craft on it would not be pretty sailing boats but commercial barges – the juggernauts of the day.

Early maps show Nash's 'Ornamental Water' as communicating with the canal at its entry to the Park on the west side and Nash recommended that "The Ornamental Water of the Park will be supplied from the Regent's Canal as in the former design, the only difference being, that it will join the Canal at the place where it leaves the Park." (10a).   The Park Commissioners made it a condition of their support for the application of the Regent's Canal Company to Government that, "The Ornamental Water proposed to be formed in Marylebone Park shall be supplied from the Canal, that such Ornamental Water shall be kept on a level with the water of the Canal, and that a sunk wall shall be erected by the Canal Company at the Commencement of the said Ornamental Water for the purpose of preventing Vessels passing up and down the Canal from entering the same." (10c).

This ornamental water – the lake in Regent's Park – must have been regarded as quite important as it features in several articles about the Regent's Canal.   John Hassell, describing the Grand Junction Canal in 1819, refers to the "Prince Regent's Canal", saying "This ramification, which is now in a fair way of being speedily completed . . .enters the Regent's Park, where it will form an ornamental sheet of water." (11), and in the Gentleman's Magazine in the same year we read "After passing through the Regent's Park, and there forming supplies for the ornamental lakes of water in the Park . . ." (12a).   It is strange, therefore, that there now appears to be no link between the two, and certainly no sunken wall preventing boats from entering the park.   The River Tyburn crosses the canal in an aqueduct to enter the lakes in Regent's Park and flows south to leave the Park near Marylebone High Street.

Planning of the canal proceeded rapidly and the first Bill was before Parliament in the summer of 1812, receiving Royal Assent on 13 July.   It is an extremely long Act "for making and maintaining a navigable Canal from the Grand Junction Canal in the Parish of Paddington, to the River Thames in the Parish of Limehouse, with a Collateral Cut in the Parish of St. Leonard, Shoreditch, in the County of Middlesex"; it covers such aspects as where the canal should get its water (and that none was to be taken from the Grand Junction Canal), how much money was to be raised and what it should charge for freight carried on the canal, its route through Regent's Park and the supply of water to the lakes therein, what may not be built by or near the canal, and the penalty to be imposed on those caught swimming in the canal (not exceeding

4

a forty-shilling fine or imprisonment for one month).

The Act diverted the route to the northern perimeter of the Park and directed that the towing path should be on the further side of the canal. Six weeks later, on 31 August, 1812, Nash submitted his Plan No. 5 to the Commissioners of His Majesty's Woods, Forest and Land Revenues saying:

"Since the adoption of the Plan No. 4, according to which I am directed to lay out and form the works carrying on in the Regents Park: several circumstances have occurred which make very considerable deviations from that Plan absolutely necessary, and others desirable. . . . the Alteration by Parliament in the course of the intended Regents Canal through the Regents Park, makes a very great alteration in that part of the Park absolutely necessary. The Canal by the Plan No. 4 was to have entered the Park in the middle of its west boundary close to the Northernmost Alpha Cottage, and to take a north easterly direction to the south west corner of the proposed Barracks; and to run along the south front of those Barracks to their eastern extremity, and from that point turn again to the north east until it entered Lord Southampton's Ground – The Canal by the Act of Parliament and with the consent of the Crown, is now to enter the Regents Park between Lords Cricket Ground and the Burial Ground of the Parish of Marylebone, and to pass through the Park along, and parallel with its north boundary – leaving the Park and entering the Ground of Lord Southampton at the same place as originally intended. This alteration of the line of the Canal will be a great improvement of the Plan No. 4 inasmuch as the privacy of the Park will not be invaded by the commerce of the Canal, and the banks will be so much elevated (nearly 25 feet) above the surface of the water, as to conceal from the Park, the traffic passing through it." (10a). This change in the route caused an awkward corner where the canal left the park towards Camden.

When reading the handwritten reports and letters sent by John Nash to the Commissioners one should appreciate the anomaly of the situation. Nash and his assistant, James Morgan, were engaged by the Commissioners responsible for the Marylebone Estate to plan and lay out the Regent's Park. Nash and Morgan were also engaged by the Regent's Canal Company to plan and construct the canal which runs through the park. Thus when Nash wrote to the Commissioners, for example, on 11 November, 1813: "I beg therefore to submit that a letter be written by the Board to the Directors of the Canal Company requiring them to deposit the soil excavated at the West end of their Canal so as to raise the ground in the valley opposite the Alpha Cottages to a foot above their Canal water" (10b) he was asking for a letter which would end up on his own desk when he was wearing another hat. The Chairman of the Regent's Canal Company, Lord Glenbervie, who also wore several hats did not fare so well. An M.P. raised the matter in the House of Commons on 1 May, 1812: "Mr. Creevey accused Lord Glenbervie, the Surveyor General, and the chief proprietor of the Regent's Canal, of making profitable agreements between himself and himself, in his respective capacities." (12b).

Negotiations for the purchase of land for the construction of the canal which should have been completed before work started were delayed by certain landowners who demanded outrageous compensation from the canal company, particularly a Mr William Agar, who in 1810 had bought land across the route of the canal. (It is noted that the 1812 Regent's Canal Act lists 'the Honourable George Charles Agar' as one of the 'Company of Proprietors of the Regent's Canal'; he probably knew the proposed route of the canal prepared by Thomas Homer some years earlier). William Agar

Councillor Agar's House, Somers Town, in 1830

subsequently became involved in a long drawn out dispute with action ranging from a Petition to the House of Lords to confrontation with the navvies by his staff. "Mr William Agar – or as he was commonly called, 'Councillor Agar', an eccentric and miserly lawyer . . ." (13) lived in Elm Grove on an estate of some seventy acres (see page 30). It was on this land that the disreputable Agar Town later sprang up; "Agars Fields had become one of the greatest sinks of filth, disease and pauperism in London" (14).

4. Building the Regent's Canal

The first meeting of the proprietors was held on 10 August, 1812 at the Freemason's Tavern at St. Giles-in-the-Fields when John Nash was appointed to be one of the Directors and his assistant, James Morgan, was appointed engineer, architect and land surveyor (15). Thomas Homer, who had originated the scheme, had no money invested but was, nevertheless, appointed superintendent (9). As none of these was experienced in canal building, prizes of fifty guineas each were offered for the best design of tunnels and of locks.

The Proprietors were particularly concerned with the construction of the tunnels, especially as a road tunnel through Highgate Hill had recently collapsed (see page 24). John Rennie, who had been responsible for the Lancaster Canal and the Kennet & Avon Canal with their fine aqueducts, had been invited to be one of the judges. Unfortunately the Highgate tunnel was being built by Rennie; he tactfully declined to serve on the panel of judges for the Regent's Canal tunnels and sought the advice of John Nash on his problem of Highgate. Nash recommended the removal of the entire tunnel and its replacement with a deep cutting spanned by a viaduct (9); the road became Highgate Archway Road, now Archway Road, and forms part of the Great North Road.

6

In the meantime the response to the advertisement for tunnel designs was a disappointment — one design submitted was a copy of a tunnel by Jessop on which the contender had worked, not realising perhaps, that Jessop had been appointed to the panel of judges in Rennie's place. In the end Morgan was instructed to prepare his own designs and these were adopted (9).

The locks presented a different problem. As water was going to be particularly short (see page 9), a lock was needed which required little, if any, water to pass a boat through it. The committee was approached in 1814 by Colonel William Congreve, an inventor who had patented a 'hydro-pneumatic double-balance lock' to achieve this (16). It consisted essentially of a pair of lock chambers alongside each other, their floors capable of being raised and lowered to lift the water level to that of the upper and the lower pound respectively. The base of each lock was, in effect, a piston operated by air trapped beneath it; the air pockets communicated with each other and through the connecting conduit was a chain, running on pulleys, linking the two pistons. Congreve believed that "the effort of one or two men in about one minute would change the level of an ordinary lock" (16). James Morgan supported the scheme but suggested that a trial lock should first be built at Hampstead Road Top Lock. Construction began in 1814 but delays occurred, mainly due to leakages, and following an accident in 1818 the Committee decided to abandon the invention and opt for conventional locks.

The building of the canal commenced on Wednesday, 14 October, 1812: "The ceremony of putting the first spade into the ground of the intended line of the Regent's Canal, took place this day. A branch of the canal is projected to extend to certain places already marked out on the Eastern side of the Regent's Park, close to the New Road, for the site of three new markets, for meat, vegetables and hay. The Act directs that the part of the Canal extending through the Regent's Park, shall be executed in twelve months. The Company have purchased 120 acres of Finchley Common, for the purpose of forming a head of water, which is to feed their canal." (12c)

Hampstead Road Top Lock with oblique bridge beyond it.
A pair of conventional locks was built when Congreve's Patent Lock failed.

The part through Regent's Park was completed by 11 November, 1813, and the stretch between Little Venice and Hampstead Road – with the exception of part of Maida Hill tunnel – by 1 June, 1814. The route chosen lay through the site chosen by Thomas Lord for his new cricket ground; in 1811 he had moved the turf from the original ground established in the area of Dorset Square to the new site and the Regent's canal company had to pay him compensation of £4,000 so that he could establish it in its present position. The Company also supplied the top soil for the cricket ground from the excavation of Maida Hill tunnel. The section of the Regent's Canal from the link with the Grand Junction Canal at Little Venice to Hampstead Road – that is the two-and-a half mile lock-free stretch – was formally opened for business on the Prince Regent's birthday, 12 August, 1816.

Another problem beset them at about this time. On 4 April, 1815 the Chairman of the Company received an anonymous letter implying that Thomas Homer had embezzled Company funds – a charge subsequently admitted by Homer who had fled the country. The funds were never recovered and subscribers had to be asked for further payments to allow construction to continue. Financial difficulties also threatened the completion of the rest of the canal. "This important work had been for some time suspended, but on August 12, 1817 (the Prince Regent's birthday), the proceedings were recommenced, in consequence of a resolution of the Commissioners for the issue of Exchequer Bills to advance the Canal Company, on loan, £200,000 in addition to £100,000 raised by the proprietors amongst themselves." (12a). The Loan Commissioners were enabled, under the Poor Employment Act of 1817, to grant Government funds for public works to provide jobs. Following the Napoleonic wars there was a large unemployment problem in Britain and, as the Act stated, "Whereas great Advantage may arise, under present Circumstances, in affording Employment for the labouring Classes of the Community, by the Advance of Exchequer Bills . . .for the carrying on of Works of a public Nature." Thus the Regent's Canal was completed by means of a job creation scheme introduced during the reign of George III.

Three further Acts of Parliament concerning the Regent's Canal reached the Statute Book while the canal was under construction, each amending the 1812 Act; in 1813 the course of the canal through Regent's Park was amended and the 1816 Act dealt largely with finance but also empowered the company to supply Thames water to the Grand Junction Canal Company (see page 11) and it also settled the dispute over Agar's land. Discussions on his claim for compensation had continued for several years, although he finally agreed a sum, the matter had to be incorporated in an Act and in Parliament there was considerable opposition to his being paid any money at all, with the result that the final settlement in May 1818 was substantially less than that to which he had previously agreed.

The fourth Act in 1819 authorised the digging of Wenlock Basin and also permitted William Horsfall to build a basin on his land near Battle Bridge. It detailed the construction of City Road Basin and allowed the Company to lay pipes into the Thames. The building of Islington tunnel was completed towards the end of 1818, and though the hoped for completion by the end of 1819 did not materialise, the grand opening of the Regent's Canal from the Grand Junction Canal at Paddington through to the Thames at Limehouse was celebrated on 1 August, 1820. The Times, on 2 August, 1820, reported:

"Yesterday being the day appointed for the formal opening of the new branch of the Regent's Canal, the Managing Committee, with Colonel Drinkwater, the Chairman, Mr Morgan, the head engineer of this most stupendous undertaking, Mr Nash, the head surveyor, Mr John Cleverly, and the other under surveyors, together with the principal proprietors, and a number of other persons of rank and respectability connected with the undertaking, assembled near Maiden-lane at about eleven o'clock, and took the water at that part of the Canal which is contiguous.   The Committee embarked on board one of the City State Barges, which had been borrowed for the occasion, and they were accompanied by several other barges, having on board bands of music, and decorated with flags and streamers in profusion.

The day being favourable, the crowds assembled to witness the ceremony were immense, particularly at the grand basin in the City-road.   The procession went under the great tunnel through Islington, where the bands of music played several national airs, and the effect produced by the reverberation of the sound was grand beyond description.   The party then proceeded to the grand basin in the City-road, where a salute was fired, and they were hailed with the loudest acclamations from the numerous crowds assembled on the shore.   After having gone round the basin, the party proceeded down the Canal to Limehouse, and in their course met with the same reception from the well-dressed persons who lined the sides of the Canal the whole distance.   At Limehouse the party stopped, and partook of a magnificent dinner."
(17).

5.   *Where the Canal got its Water*

The Regent's Canal drops eighty-six feet through twelve locks from Little Venice to Limehouse and the proprietors of the Grand Junction Canal, with which it links, were well aware that a lock on the Regent's Canal would need 56,000 gallons of water every time it was filled.   Following representations to Parliament, the 1812 Act laid down: "Whereas the said Canal . . .will partly be on a lower level than the said Grand Junction Canal or navigable Cut . . .a Regulating Pound, or Stop Lock shall be built, and the Water in the Lock shall be at all times at least Six Inches above the top Water of the said navigable Cut."

Initially it was hoped that the Congreve "hydro-pneumatic doulbe-balance lock" would be the solution but the idea has to be abandoned and conventional locks were decided upon (see page 7).   However paired locks were installed throughout the canal and these had inter-connecting sluices between the two chambers so that when they were worked together — like side-ponds — up to half of the 56,000 gallons could be saved.   The paddle was raised by means of a rack and pinion on a post between the locks (see page 20).   It was essential that a supply of water for the Regent's Canal was obtained;   "The Company have purchased 120 acres of Finchley Common for the purpose of forming a head of water, which is to feed their canal".   (see page 7). This involved nine miles of feeder which was to connect, also, with another reservoir between Muswell Hill and Highgate.   The 1812 Act supported this proposal and required that the Stop Lock should be built to the west of Edgware Road and kept filled with water from the reservoir at Finchley or from the Thames.   Stop gates were built at the junction of the canals under Warwick Avenue Bridge (see page   ); on survey, however, it was discovered that the reservoirs would supply sufficient water for only two locksful a day so this plan had to be abandoned.

The only source of water, therefore, was the Thames and two schemes were considered.   One was to build a 2½ mile headway from the Thames at Chelsea to a

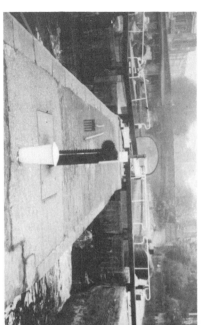

Above: City Road Locks 1835

Below: 1972 The Central paddle was still present and both locks were in use at the time.

Buried pipe in Towing Path near City Road Basin

Flap valve unearthed in Towing Path by Wharf Road Bridge

pump at Paddington which would raise the water into the canal. The cost of this was estimated to be £31,300. The alternative was to back-pump the water from the Thames at Limehouse, past groups of locks, through pipes under the towing path, estimated to cost £33,700. The cheaper Chelsea scheme was decided upon but before it could be implemented, a clause in the Regent's Canal Act prohibited the erection of "any steam engine whatsoever, in the Parish of Paddington". Undeterred, the proprietors built the pump at Chelsea to push the Thames water into the canal at Paddington, but this too ran into difficulties. The Grand Junction Canal Company had a subsidiary, the Grand Junction Waterworks Company which supplied domestic water to parts of west London and it was not prepared to have the canal water contaminated by the filthy Thames of that time, in which "Foul excreta-soaked mud festered on the flats at low tide, and, at the flood, horrible muck was borne upstream in ever-increasing loads. . . .Fish barely survived; birds began to retreat." (18). Eventually an agreement was reached whereby the Grand Junction Waterworks Company would accept the water from the Chelsea pumphouse for purification, and the Regent's Canal Company would buy its water from the Grand Junction Canal. This proved to be an expensive arrangement and an alternative source of water was sought.

At first there seemed to be no evidence that the back-pumping scheme was ever undertaken. I met Joe Young, a canal worker who had joined the Regent's Canal Company in November, 1918 — he recalls that the bells were ringing and the maroons sounding on the day he started work, but he thinks that that was likely to be associated with the Armistice — and he was in no doubt that pumps were operating at certain locks (19). Proof came when, in 1979, the Central Electricity Generating Board was laying its cables under the towing path and unearthed a twenty-four inch cast-iron pipe at one of the sites described by Joe. The pipe ran from below Sturts Lock to above City Road Lock and there was evidence of a pumping station beside Sturts Lock with connections to the pipe. Close to Wharf Road Bridge was a chamber in the pipe containing a metal flap which would allow water to pass to above City Road Lock but would prevent it from flowing back again. Further evidence was found in an article which appeared in an 1885 magazine. The writer, who is describing a trip he took on a barge through London, comments "And while our odorous barge is passing through Acton's Lock we will go ashore and look about. An engine is snorting alongside the lock — 'a stationary engine', explains our skipper, ' 'cos it's always there' — and it pumps water into the canal when needed. There is one at nearly every lock below this to the Thames." (20)

The sites of all the back-pumping stations have now been established. One stood at Regent's Canal Dock adjacent to the barge lock — now blocked up — and it drew water from a culvert which extended some sixty yards into the Thames. From here the water was pumped round the Regent's Canal Basin, and the pipe crosses Commercial Road Locks, attached to the bridge on its south side, to the towing path. A short distance on the other side of the bridge can be seen a control valve and inspection cover in a brick housing in the undergrowth beside the towing path. The pipe continued to above Mile End Lock. The other pumps stood beside Old Ford Lock, Sturts Lock, St. Pancras Lock, and Kentish Town Lock.

In investigating these sites and the pipe runs, it was essential to establish that the pipes did not belong to the London Hydraulic Power Company which supplied water under pressure to factories and machinery in a large area of London. From 1852 pumping stations were being built all over London to pump water under pressure

11

to operate machinery; the first was built by the Regent's Canal Company at Lime-house Dock and then more were built in the other docks, and at railway sidings near the canal. The many hydraulic power networks, each serving a small amount of equipment, proved uneconomical and this led, in 1871, to the foundation of the London Hydraulic Power Company. This energy was used to operate presses, wagon hoists, safety curtains in West End Theatres, the bascules of Tower Bridge, and even the lifts at the London Hospital in Whitechapel as well as the lock gates, the swing bridge and some of the cranes around Regent's Canal Dock. The pressurised water was supplied through 184 miles of pipes until the last pumping station closed in 1977. A map in the Tower Hamlets Local History Collection shows the sites of the pumping stations and the routes of the mains and none ran under the towing path of the Regent's Canal, even though one station took its water from the canal at City Road Basin (see page 55). The main did cross Commercial Road Bridge, but it was in a 7-inch iron pipe buried in the roadway so the large pipe to be seen attached to the bridge is certainly not that used by the London Hydraulic Power Company. That Company, incidentally, has been bought by Mercury Communications for their telephone network and detailed information on the positon of the pipes has been obtained from its staff.

When the Hertford Union Canal was built in 1830 between the River Lee Navigation and the Regent's Canal at Old Ford Lock an arrangement was made that water from the Lee should be pumped into the Regent's Canal. This happened for a while but proved unsatisfactory and was soon discontinued. In 1835 the Regent's Canal Company took over a concession from the Grand Junction Canal Company to build the Brent Reservoir by damming the River Brent; few people who take their recreation on the Welsh Harp north of the North Circular Road realise that it was built by a canal company and that the reservoir can still supply the canal with water through the feeder which enters the Paddington Arm near Harlesdon. Cast iron posts around the reservoir identify it as the property of the Regent's Canal Company.

All the water difficulties encountered by the Regent's Canal Company were resolved when it acquired the Grand Junction Canal and several canals around Birmingham to form the Grand Union Canal on 1 January, 1929; the following year further canals in the Leicestershire area were added to the amalgamation providing the Grand Union Canal Company with a route from London to Birmingham and also to the River Trent. Officially, therefore, there is now no Regent's Canal but a part of the Grand Union through London. Nevertheless several of the components of the union are still identified by their earlier names, such as the Soar Navigation and the Erewash Canal.

THE REGENT'S CANAL AND ITS WATER SUPPLY

based on a "Plan of the Intended Canal – 1811"
with water supply proposals added.

Note a) alternative route suggested to the north of the tunnel through Maida Hill
   b) route through the centre of Mary le bone (Regent's) Park
   c) "Intended Feeder" and "Intended Headway"
   d) Canal joining the Thames at Limehouse with no basin shown.

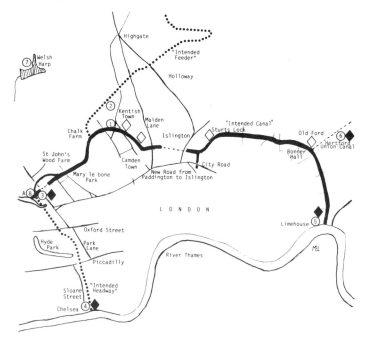

SUMMARY OF WATER SUPPLY PROPOSALS

A   The 1812 Act prohibited the use of water from the Grand Junction Canal.
1   Congreve Lock tested and failed at Hampstead Road Lock
2   Feeder from Finchley Common would not supply sufficient water
3   Pumphouse planned at Paddington thwarted when steam engines banned in the Parish of Paddington
4   Pumphouse built at Chelsea but its use prohibited to avoid contamination of canal with Thames water. Supply agreed to Grand Junction Waterwoks Co. and Regent's Canal Co. authorised to purchase water from G.J. Canal Co.
5   Backpumping of water from Thames up length of Canal
6   Water pumped from Lee tried but abandoned
7   Brent Reservoir – Welsh Harp – built 1835
8   Amalgamation of Grand Junction and Regent's Canals in 1929 to form the Grand Union Canal

13

6. How it Fared

In its first full year of operation the Regent's Canal Company was able to report the carriage of nearly 195,000 tons and this increased steadily; in the financial year ending April 1829 it carried over 495,000 tons, and in 1834 this had risen to nearly 625,000 which earned £28,930 in tolls (6b). The Tonnage Rates, listed in the 1812 Regent's Canal Act, included 6d a ton toll "for all Goods, Wares, Merchandize and other Things, which shall enter the Mouths of the said Canal" and an additional 4/- a ton conveyed the entire length of the canal. "Lime, Lime-stone, Chalk, Bricks, Tiles, Slates, Lead, Iron, Brass, Copper, Tin, Platina, Stone and Timber of every kind" and "Coals, Coke and other materials" were charged at the rate of 3/- a ton and Manure cost 1/6d a ton.

The slope into Euston Station – 1837. A stationary engine, between the two stacks, lowers the carriages on wires into the station, the bridge over the canal is seen to the left of the stacks and beyond them is the smoke of a waiting locomotive.

A bottleneck soon became apparent at Islington Tunnel caused by the need to leg boats through it (see page 26) and the company made it compulsory for boatmen to hire licensed leggers for a fixed fee (6c). In 1826 a tug was introduced (see page 27) and though this took half an hour to tow four fifty-ton barges through (21), it was quicker than legging. It must have been an unpleasant journey; about a century later, in 1924, a silent film entitled "Barging Through London" included the captions "This gloomy cavern is three-quarters of a mile in length, passes under the New River, and takes us half-an-hour to be tugged through" and "Nearly gassed – but nearly through". An article in the Daily Telegraph on 27 June, 1925 commented "There is no towing path through the tunnel, and, consequently, powerful tugs were used to tow the barges through. The Islington Tunnel is 1,000 yards in length, and it was found that difficulty occurred owing to the length of time which it took to accomplish the journey, and also the danger from fumes emitted from the tug funnel. The difficulty has been overcome by installing a craft fitted with a winding drum around which

14

passes a cable, secured at either end of the tunnel." (33)

The Company's problems began, however, only twelve years after the opening of the canal when the first railway from the Midlands reached London; just as the canals had vied with each other to provide better transport between Birmingham and London (see page 2) so the railways entered the competition. Robert Stephenson built the London and Birmingham Railway in 1831–32, following the same route as the Grand Junction Canal; it became common practice for railways to run alongside canals because the railways, like the canals, needed relatively level ground (the locomotives could not tolerate hills) and the railway companies wished to attract the trade built up by the canal companies along their course. In 1852 the London and York railway was opened to a temporary terminus in Maiden Lane – or York Road as it was renamed (now York Way) – and the Midland Railway reached London in 1868.

All these railway companies wanted their main passenger stations on the New Road (see page 3), but it meant that they all had to cross the Regent's Canal which ran to the north of it. In 1837 Stephenson took his railway over the Canal and the line then sloped down to Euston Station, a slope up which the early locomotives could not pull the carriages. The locomotives therefore waited at the top and the carriages were lowered down into the station by means of wires operated by a stationary engine beside the canal (see page 29). One of two circular engine sheds, built in 1847 by Robert Stephenson, remains at Chalk Farm, the Round House, which has more recently been used for entertainment. The London to York Railway became the Great Northern Railway and its lines went under the canal; unfortunately it was very prone to flooding and only a few years ago during a heavy rain storm trains in and out of Kings Cross were disrupted by water on the lines just outside the station. In 1868, therefore, the Midland Railway was taken over the canal and St Pancras Station was built up seventeen feet to avoid an incline into the station. When eventually locomotives were built strong enough to pull the carriages up the slope, they made such a noise that it is reported that horses towing the barges along the canal bolted and fell into the canal (see page 19); this sounds like a story invented by the canal owners who did not like the competition from the railways, but it seems to have happened often enough for the Regent's Canal Company to build horse ramps on either side of railway bridges so that the horses could be led up out of the water.

In September, 1845, the Directors of the Regent's Canal Company received an offer to convert the canal into a railway from Paddington to City Road Basin. Their reluctance to accept the offer was changed to an enthusiastic approval when the offer was increased to one million pounds and it was proposed to call the line the Regent's Canal Railway. Four months later the railway company failed to raise the money and the scheme fell through. Several further attempts were made and on 23 February, 1823, an advertisement appeared in the Daily News "Issue of £1,275,000 Stock (Canal Capital). Regent's Canal City and Docks Railway Company, created for the purchase of the entire undertaking of the existing Regent's Canal Company ...". This was the last such offer to fail and by the end of the century new plans were introduced to improve the waterway.

Traffic on the canals declined and whereas the railways could be selective about the goods they accepted for carriage, this option was not open to the struggling canals. As reported in the Mail on Monday 5 October, 1874 "At about 3 a.m. a train of six light barges, of which the first was a steamer, left the City Road Wharf of the Grand Junction Canal Company in the City Road." In the middle was a barge called

Tilbury, "The cargo consisted chiefly of sugar and other miscellaneous articles such as nuts, straw-boards, coffee, and some two or three barrels of petroleum, and about five tons of gunpowder." The gun-powder was destined for quarries in the Nottingham area. They reached Macclesfield Bridge in Regent's Park at 4.55 a.m. when Tilbury exploded demolishing the bridge. The canal was reopened only four days later and when subsequently the bridge was rebuilt, at the expense of the Grand Junction Carrying Company who owned the Tilbury, the columns cast in Coalbrookdale were used again (see page 38).

It is no coincidence that the Explosives Act, regulating the transport of explosive substances, received Royal Assent on 14 June, 1875, within nine months of this disaster. A leading article in the Illustrated London News on Saturday 10 October, 1874, called for a review of goods carried through the centre of cities on the canals and commented "it behoves us to be thankful that a much worse fate did not befall the metropolis on Friday morning. The qualifying and mitigating circumstances which attended the explosion wonderfully contracted the range of its destructive power. It happened when most of the inhabitants of the metropolis were abed, and thereby sheltered from the worst effects of the momentary blast. Few people were about. The neighbourhood in which the accident occurred was one of the most open suburbs of London. At the precise spot at which it took place the canal runs through a considerable cutting, and the banks on either hand served to give a primarily vertical direction to the atmospheric wave. An eminent authority on such matters is reported to have said, 'That dip saved London.' At any rate, the loss of life was comparatively small, three persons only being known to have been killed." (22). The train of barges must have passed through Islington Tunnel soon after three o'clock in the morning.

In common with all the canals in the country, more and more traffic was lost to the railways, and then later to the roads. During the 1914 war the Regent's Canal was taken over by the Board of Trade and soon after the war the Company began reviewing its revenue. By 1926 consideration had been given to the possibility of amalgamating with the Grand Junction and several other canals to form the Grand Union Canal, and this was achieved on 1 April, 1929. In 1948 the canal passed to the control of the British Transport Commission and in January 1963 the British Waterways Board assumed responsibility for it.

The Daily Telegraph, in June 1925, reported on "some interesting trials carried out along the Regent's and Grand Junction Canals for the purpose of determining the value of tractor haulage as compared with horse haulage of barges. It is too early to decide whether or not the advantage lies with the tractor, because insufficient time has elapsed to obtain statistics as to the cost of running. So far as actual results are concerned, it is interesting to learn that the tractor was able to tow two barges a specified distance in one-half the time that would be occupied by horses" (33). The last horse towed a barge in 1956 (9). The canal is now used principally by pleasure craft, including privately owned boats of all shapes and sizes, and hired boats; trip boats provide an opportunity for people to enjoy the canal without any of the work involved. The only working boats are those owned by the British Waterways Board, used for maintaining the fabric of the canal and for clearing rubbish out of the water, and craft used by contractors, for instance when bridges need painting or repair or when work is being undertaken on the towing path.

THE REGENT'S CANAL TODAY

The Canal and its environment

The Regent's Canal is about 8½ miles long from Paddington to the Thames at Limehouse and it drops some 86 feet between Little Venice and Limehouse Basin through twelve locks. It is a 'broad' canal — the locks and bridge holes will admit a pair of narrow-boats alongside each other — and its depth is about four feet. The main line of the canal is spanned by 36 road bridges, 9 foot-bridges, 10 railways and two tunnels. In one place, at Hampstead Road Lock, the towing path is on the opposite side, the horse crosses the canal over the oblique bridge and the towing rope has to be disconnected to allow the barge to pass under the bridge. However when the horse crosses back, over Hampstead Road (now Chalk Farm Road) Bridge, the arrangement is such that the horse may remain attached to the barge while it returns to the towing path on the left of the canal. Some of the early brick bridges show the asymmetry characteristic of the canals; the arch rises from the water in a smooth curve over the canal to above the towing path. Here the curve is adjusted to provide sufficient head-room for horses to walk through it. The names of many of the bridges, basins and locks commemorate the original owners of the land through which the canal was dug, for instance George Thornton, William Horsfall and Joe Acton.

One feature of the Regent's Canal which has been evident in the past two decades has been the improvements made — by a variety of local organisations, by the British Waterways Board and by riparian Councils — to the environment of the canal. In 1964 the London County Council, Inland Waterways Association and other local Councils and voluntary bodies considered possible improvements to the Little Venice area and in 1967 an important report "The Regent's Canal — a Policy for its Future" was published by the Regent's Canal Group, a body composed of societies interested in the waterways in Paddington, Islington, St Pancras and Hackney, together with the London Branch of the Inland Waterways Association and the Civic Trust. The report was featured in the Illustrated London News dated 20 May, 1967, in which it was said of the Canal that litter and rubbish disfigured the banks and polluted the water; its towing path was closed to the public, except for the half mile between Hampstead Road Locks and the Zoo for which British Waterways Board issued permits at 2s 6d a year. It seems now that many of the plans were over optimistic; one scheme described in detail was the development of Haggerston Basin up to Whiston Road as an amenity with moorings for boats on it (the section beyond Whiston Road had been filled in after the war to provide a public park). Unfortunately the entire basin has since been obliterated and built on.

In the Autumn of 1969 the London Canals Consultative Committee published "London's Canal — Its Past, Present and Future" with a similar description of the canal scene then: "A number of original warehouses and factories, complete with docks and basins, still remain, some of them disused and derelict. Many have been replaced by modern industrial buildings which no longer have a use for the canal. Together, old and new, they form bold 'wallscapes' on either side of brick, concrete and glass from which come the sometimes puzzling hissings and hummings of industry. But there are also pockets of canalside industry where old workshops and warehouses, having turned their backs on the canal, stack refuse and scrap materials beside it, marring what could, very often, be a pleasant scene. Some bridges crossing the canal have advertisement hoardings on either side concealing it so effectively from view that many Londoners do not know that there is a canal; others are less closed in and, from the canal, it is possible to glimpse tall lorries and the occasional bus. Often the canal hides behind walls and old fencing." (23)

It is difficult to realise that the junk heaps, piles of tarpaulin and corrugated iron, broken fences, sheds draped with sacking and plastic sheeting and dilapidated towing paths which were so prominent in the early sixties are no longer to be seen along the water's edge. So much seems to be happening along the canal that any description of what is to be seen is likely to become out of date fairly quickly. Local authorities have done a lot. Parks and seating areas have been opened overlooking the water, and new housing estates, separated from the canal by fencing rather than walls, are being built. Even the bridges are now allowing views of the water and the advertisement hoardings, complained of in the Consultative Committee booklet, are gone. Industries alongside the canal are also beginning to take an interest in the water. Canteens are being built overlooking it and grass and seating are appearing on its banks. There is still much to be done but the outlook is optimistic.

Recently the British Waterways Board appointed a London Canals Project Officer to liaise with bodies interested in the Regent's Canal, and in 1985 the Board commissioned the London Wildlife Trust to carry out a wildlife survey of the Canal to identify areas in need of special protection and places where new planting and landscape schemes would benefit the environment; BWB is implementing many of the management proposals. Shrubs and trees are also being planted along the Canal by the Hoxton Trust.

Horse Ramp

The Towing Path

The first Council to open up the towing path to the public was the City of Westminster in 1968. Camden followed so by 1974 it was possible to walk beside the canal from Maida Hill to Islington Tunnels. Islington and Hackney then introduced schemes for the improvement of landscaping of the towing path and in May, 1982, the London Branch of the Inland Waterways Association held a Canalway Festival at Mile End to celebrate the completion of the work in Tower Hamlets; the entire length of the towing path along the Regent's Canal had been cleared, the pathway improved and access provided at numerous places along it. Several of the authorities placed cast metal notices describing features to be seen along the Canal but nearly all of them have since disappeared, probably removed by vandals.

The towing path itself is now in fairly good condition; when the Central Electricity Generating Board laid its cables under the towing path between Maida Hill Tunnel and the junction with the Hertford Union, it left the pathway in good repair, though some of the paving stones are rocky and, in wet weather, have been known to squirt oily water onto ones shoes. The CEGB also built pumping stations to pump canal water alongside the cables to keep them cool; most of the stations are in yellow brick, the exception being that by the Pirate's Castle where the pump-house has been built to match the castle ramparts. British Waterways Board sells a lot of water to industry for cooling purposes, and it is probably the only supplier that can sell something on condition that it is given back.

Horse ramps can still be seen as inlets into the towing path adjacent to the canal, with a cobbled slope up from the bottom of the canal. They were provided by the Regent's Canal Company so that when horses towing barges slipped and fell into the canal they could be led back up to the towing path. When the railways came to London and crossed the canal, a horse ramp was built on either side of every railway bridge; it is said that the horses were frightened by the early locomotives and frequently bolted. The canal company also issued instructions to all boatmen that they were not to use the horse ramps for washing their horses. Some of the ramps have been obliterated entirely, and others have been rebuilt so their original purpose is obscured; some twenty one remain and are shown on the maps alongside the description of the Canal.

Locks

The locks on the Regent's Canal are all double locks, but in 1973 the British Waterways Board launched a scheme to convert the second lock — with the exception of that at Hampstead Road — into a weir. Until this was done, boaters could use the canal only when lock-keepers were on duty, normally 8.0 a.m. to 5.0 p.m. on Monday to Friday and 8.0 till noon on Saturday, but during the summer months they were opened on a few Sundays too. B.W.B. staff had to regulate the flow of water down the Regent's Canal to avoid flooding. The weirs have obviated this risk and the locks may now be used at any time.

The paddle gear on the locks is of the conventional Grand Union type. The Paddles are squares of timber which prevent water from flowing through apertures until they are raised. The apertures are below water-level, either in the gates themselves — gate paddles — or through conduits in the brickwork to bypass the gates — ground paddles. Gate paddles were provided on the lower gates and both ground and gate paddles on the upper gates. However, on the Regent's Canal the gate paddles on the upper gates have been disconnected. A possible reason for this is that when a lock is being filled, it is possible to open the gate paddles too soon — before the ground paddles are opened — which could flood a boat in the lock, making it dangerous for boaters who are not familiar with the hazard. On some locks, too, the method of raising the paddles has been modified. The conventional rack and pinion system can be heavy to operate and has also been the subject of criticism from a safety point of view. British Waterways Board therefore introduced hydraulic paddle gear on some locks; these are much easier to operate, but a lot of canal users think they can be dangerous as they cannot be lowered rapidly in an emergency — such emergencies can arise, when the water is being lowered in a lock, if a boat was tied tightly to bollards when the lock was full, or if a boat is too close to the upper gates where the stern gear can be damaged on the sill. The Board carried out a survey among canal users and its own maintenance staff in 1985 and is considering its future policy. Examples of hydraulic paddle gear can be seen along the canal.

When the locks were built, each pair was interconnected so that, when worked together, water could be run from the full chamber into the 'empty' one until they were both half full to save water (see page 9). The conduit, below water level, was closed with a paddle which could be raised by means of a rack and pinion on the island separating the locks. This paddle gear has been removed from most locks, but can be seen still on Hampstead Road Top Lock and Johnsons Lock.

Visiting the Regent's Canal

Practically all the boats on the canal are pleasure craft, most of them privately owned. Moorings are provided at Blomfield Road, near Lisson Grove, at St Pancras Cruising Club, in Battlebridge, Wenlock and Kingsland Basins. Boats from the River Lee Navigation — where there are four cruising clubs — use the canal on the way to the Grand Union Canal and most of them prefer this route to that on the Thames tideway when aiming for the upper Thames. There will be some hired boats, but there are no boat hire firms on the Regent's Canal. Riparian Councils own boats, mainly for their youth work, including "Victoria" (Westminster) and "Tarporley" (Camden) and a frequent visitor is "Challenge", a broad beamed boat designed for use by handicapped with facilities for wheel-chairs, operated by the Dockland Trust; its normal mooring is on the Hertford Union Canal.

Visiting boats may tie up anywhere on the Canal — except within the area of the Zoo — and the CEGB, when it was laying its cables under the towing path, provided bollards, particularly near locks. Boaters therefore do not need to hammer mooring stakes into the towing path, with the possible hazard of damaging the cables. BWB sanitary station keys fit the toilets and chemical disposal unit at St Pancras lock and they also fit the gates from the towing path so that, when mooring for the night, it is possible to return to the boat when the towing path is locked. There is a temporary mooring — limited to 48 hours — between Regent's Park Road and Gloucester Avenue.

Fishing is available for members of the angling clubs which are granted fishing rights along sections of the canal, or day tickets are obtainable from the bailiffs; gudgeon, roach, perch, bream, pike and tench are said to abound. Cycling permits may be obtained from British Waterways Board, but motor cycling and horse-riding are not allowed. Swimming in the canal is forbidden.

20

The public is being invited to see the Regent's Canal in a number of ways. Jason's Trip from Blomfield Road has been running to Hampstead Road Lock and back since 1951, sometimes using the motor boat "Jason" on its own, sometimes towing its butty 'Serpens''. The Waterways Bus service started in 1959; the purpose-built broad beamed "Water Buffalo" or one of the converted traditional working narrowboats "Perseus" or "Gardenia" leaves Little Venice and Camden, stopping at the Zoo, every weekend throughout the year and daily from March to October. Jenny Wren Cruises have been running since 1968 and the Fair Lady Cruising Restaurant, since 1972. Jenny Wren sails regularly from below Hampstead Road Lock to Little Venice between March and October and Fair Lady serves dinners Monday to Saturday, and Sunday lunch, throughout the year. The booking office and entrance is on Camden High Street next to Hampstead Road Bridge. The companies can arrange private party bookings. From 1977 the London Branch of the Inland Waterways Association has been arranging guided walks along the Regent's Canal, starting at Camden Town Underground Station at 2.30 p.m. on the first Sunday of every month and at 6.15 p.m. on the third Tuesday evening of June, July and August; walks to Paddington alternate with walks to Islington. The London Waterbus Company now operates a 'Limehouse Trip' during the summer months, starting at Camden Lock and reaching Limehouse basin at lunchtime, returning by way of the River Lee and the Hertford Union Canal.

Increasing numbers of people are being introduced to the Regent's Canal. Some of them are Londoners who did not realise that a canal lay so close to the City, and others are visitors from Britain and abroad who seem to be fascinated to discover this strip of history running through the Capital.

Author giving commentary on 'Water Buffalo' on a 'Limehouse Trip'.

The Regent's Canal

Tour of the Grand Junction Canal by John Hassell, 1819, p.6

"A short distance to the left of Paddington, are the Grand Junction Waterworks, which now partly supply the west end of the town. Paddington-green was formerly celebrated for possessing some of the noblest elm trees in Middlesex, and has a tasteful little church in its centre. From hence the road leads by the side of the canal, on the right of which we are brought into view of the connection of the Prince Regent's Canal with that of the Grand Junction. This ramification, which is now in a fair way of being speedily completed, commences with a lock at the first bridge, and after passing through a short tunnel, under the Edgware road, it enters the Regent's Park, where it will form an ornamental sheet of water. Passing from thence in an easterly direction, it crosses the Hampstead and Highgate roads; at the former of which places is a curious engine for weighing the tonnage in the boats which are to navigate its surface. After passing the Kentish-town road, the canal enters the grounds of Mr Agar, at the back of St Pancrass church and Battle bridge, where a large basin is forming as a depot for articles of consumption, such as coals &c. which will be found highly convenient for the inhabitants. Running in a parallel line with Pentonville high road, it enters the grand tunnel under Islington, in the front of White Conduit House, and passes out again by an excavation into Mr Rhodes's fields, from thence to Hackney, and under the Mile-end road into the Thames."

The Courier, Thursday evening, September 21, 1820

"The Regent's Canal

. . .The Regent's Canal is one of the works for which the public are indebted to Mr Nash, by whom it was originally projected, and under whose direction it has been carried on — through a multitude of difficulties which could only have been surmounted by great ability, activity, and perseverance — to its final completion. It was begun in 1813 and opened on the 1st of August last. The expence, which amounts to about £600,000, has been exceedingly swelled by the extravagant price at which the land required has been obliged to be purchased, and by the many litigious actions which the company of subscribers were called upon, during the progress of the work, to defend.

Upon the utility of the Canal system in general, it is needless now to expatiate: of the advantages that will flow from this in particular, time alone can enable us to judge with any degree of accuracy. When the enormous expence of carting heavy articles from the wharfs on the banks of the river to the northern side of the town, including the adjacent villages, is considered, it appears quite reasonable to believe that much must be gained by water carriage; for it is known that the power of one horse applied to a floating weight, is equal to the strength of thirty, drawing the same on wheels. The average charge, as an example, for conveying manure by this Canal is tenpence per ton; gravel, chalk, lime, bricks, and iron, about one shilling; coals, lead, and copper, sixteen pence. To the inhabitants, therefore, of Hampstead, Kentish Town, Highgate, Hornsey, Tottenham, Hackney, &c. and also, of the parishes of Marylebone and Paddington, this mode of communication with the Thames must prove highly beneficial."

The Gentleman's Magazine and Historical Chronicle, Vol.98, ii; October, 1828, p.297

"Limehouse derives its name from an immense number of lime-trees with which, in former times, the place abounded. . . .The Lea Cut and the Regent's Canal both enter the Thames at Limehouse; the former was executed in 1772 for the purpose of obtaining a more direct communication between the Pool and the River Lea, which it joins at Bromley. The latter may be considered a modern public improvement, and exhibits many features of skill and ingenuity well worth the attention of the engineer. Its route is traced through nine parishes, and it is in length eight miles; its mean width is 37½ feet. It rises 84 feet by means of twelve locks, is crossed by thirty-seven bridges, passes by means of a tunnel (upwards of half a mile in length) under the New River, and part of Islington, and by another tunnel (a quarter of a mile in length) at Paddington, communicates with the Grand Junction Canal. It was executed under the direction of Mr Morgan, Civil Engineer.

The foundation of St. Anne's Church, which was one of the fifty appointed to be erected in the reign of Queen Anne, was commenced in 1712, but the building altogether was not completed until 1729. It was consecrated by the Lord Bishop of London in 1730.

The Architect, Nicholas Hawksmoor, one of Sir Christopher Wren's pupils, has in this, as well as in the church of St. George-in-the-East, exhibited a style remarkable for its solidity of appearance and singularity of design.

The length of this church from east to west is 145 feet; its breadth 78 feet; height from the ground to the large cornice which runs round the church, 50 feet; and the whole height, from the pavement to the top of the tower, 183 feet. It is of Portland Stone, and cost £38,000."

St Pancras News — 20 August, 1859

"Excursions on the Regent's Canal

Persons desirous of taking a trip from Camden Town to Paddington, should avail themselves of the opportunity offered by the swift little barge packets, that have been placed on the above Canal for the conveyance of passengers. The boats are 72 feet long and are drawn by two horses. They stop several times on their journey and the charge is 6d."

Camden and St Pancras Chronicle — Friday 9 September, 1977

"A sad and soggy tale
CAMDEN'S AMAZING UNDERWATER MAYOR
by Kevin Clarke

Camden mayor Bob Humphreys really made a splash when he visited a Camden canoe club summer project on the Regent's Canal. He was cautiously negotiating the gap between shore and ship when suddenly the waters opened up and swallowed him — chain, badge and all.

Embarrassed onlookers watched — half-amused, half-alarmed — as the mayor disappeared in a swirling mass of bubbles. They gaped, wide-eyed with amazement, as the mayoral head gently bobbed to the surface.

His worship, struggling beneath the weight of his hefty gold chain, was soon hauled ashore by helping hands. Wet and weary he hurried to his waiting car — drenched, dripping and doing his best to look dignified. Fortunately his £5,000 civic chain and his specs were safe."

"Mayor Splashes Out
— and he's the only one in the drink.

This is the incident the whole of Camden is talking about — the moment the mayor took an undignified dip in the Regent's Canal.

The Mayor's day, as guest of the Camden canoe club, was a washout. And his worship was not amused at the time. But like a good sport he admitted afterwards he could see the funny side of it.

Mayor Bob has a reputation for being up to his neck in work. This time he was totally immersed."

Islington Tunnel

At the first meeting of the proprietors of the Regent's Canal on 10 August, 1812, special attention was given to the design of the proposed tunnels. They were no doubt aware of an incident involving a road tunnel through Highgate Hill (see page 6):

Old and New London, part V, by Edward Walford, c1877, p.394

". . .a scheme was projected to construct a tunnel through the London clay at Highgate Hill, for the purpose of making a more easy communication between Holloway and Finchley. The attempt, however, failed, and the result was the construction of the open cutting which forms the present Highgate Archway Road. The failure appears to have arisen, in a great measure, from the want of experience on the part of the engineers who had charge of the work, more especially as they had such very difficult and heavy ground to work in as the London clay. The tunnel was nearly completed when it fell in with a terrific crash, in April, 1812, fortunately before the workmen had commenced their labour for the day. The idea of forming the tunnel, therefore, was ultimately abandoned, and the present arch constructed in its stead. The toll which was levied upon passengers along this road was of its kind unique, for not only was a toll levied upon the drivers of horses and vehicles, but one penny was also levied on foot passengers, sixpence was the toll upon every horse drawing."

The Gentleman's Magazine and Historical Chronicle, Vol.89 ii; August, 1819, p.105

"Mr Urban, June 3
    The tunnel formed for the Regent's Canal under the hill at Pentonville, in the parish of Islington, having excited a considerable degree of public curiosity, I request you to insert in your useful Miscellany a View of its Mouth, surmounted with a Prospect of the celebrated Tea-house, called White Conduit House, with the shattered

Plate I – Islington Tunnel

remains of the old Conduit, to which it owes its name (seen in the centre of the view). The distant objects on the left, are Islington Church and Workhouse (see Plate I.)"

"The Regent's Canal is to connect the Grand Junction Canal with the Thames. This important work had been for some time suspended, but on the 12th August, 1817 (the Prince Regent's Birth-day), the proceedings were recommenced, in consequence of a resolution of the Commissioners for the issue of Exchequer Bills, to advance the Canal Company, on loan, £200,000, in addition to £100,000 raised by the proprietors amongst themselves.

After passing through the Regent's Park, and there forming supplies for the ornamental lakes of water in the Park, it runs nearly in a straight direction across the Hampstead and Kentish-town Roads to the tunnel, as shown in the view. From the Eastern end of the tunnel the line passes along pasturage-fields to the inn called the Rosemary-branch, a little to the Westward of which, a branch will be taken off, and carried across the City-road (over which will be erected a handsome bridge); and the Canal then proceeds across the Kingsland and Agastone-roads to the Cambridge-heath-roads, and then to Mile-end-road, across the Commercial-road; and finally terminates in the North bank of the Thames at Limehouse, being altogether a distance of 8 3/4 miles.

The estimated revenue of the Canal, when completed is £60,000 per annum, and the expence of maintenance and management (exclusive of prime cost) is estimated at £10,000 per annum, leaving the annual sum of £50,000 for interest and dividends. The whole line is now so nearly complete, that it is expected to be opened in a few months.   Yours, &c. T.B."

On the Canal – Household Words, Vol.18, No.422, Saturday 11 September, 1858; p.291

Legging through a tunnel.

"About one o'clock in the morning we reached the Islington tunnel, and here we are enlightened as to another process of barge propulsion, called legging. A couple of strong thick boards, very like in shape to tailors' sleeve-boards, but twice the size, are hooked on to places formed on each side of the barge, near the head, from which they project like two raised oars. On these two narrow, insecure platforms, the two venturesome boatmen lie on their backs, holding on by grasping the board underneath, and with their legs, up to the waist, hanging over the water. A lantern, placed at the head of the barge, serves to light the operation which consists in moving the Stourport through the black tunnel, by a measured side-step against the slimy, glistening walls; the right foot is first planted in a half-slanting direction, and the left foot is constantly brought over with a sweep to take the vacated place, until the right can recover its footing, like the operation known as 'hands over' by young ladies who play upon the piano in a showy and gymnastic manner. The Stourport, steered by its commander, Captain Randle, walks through the tunnel in the dead of the night, by the aid of its four stout legs, and its four heavily hob-nailed boots, that make a full echoing sound upon the walls like the measured clapping of hands, but disturb not the sleeping inmates of houses and kitchens under which they pass; many of whom, perhaps, are utterly ignorant of the black and barge-loaded Styx that flows beneath them."

Newspaper paragraph, c1880 (Tower Hamlets Local History Collection)

"Complaints respecting the impure and offensive condition of the Regent's Canal having become numerous and urgent, the sanitary authorities of Mile End recently determined to make a personal inspection of the canal. To that end a barge was hired, and laden with sandwiches, bottled beer, and vestrymen, it started from the Regent's Canal Basin. . . .the eastern end of the Islington tunnel was achieved. Here several vestrymen were daunted by the gloomy appearance of the entrance, and in spite of the boisterous jeers of their colleagues, they landed and were seen no more. The remainder of the crew boldly piloted the barge into the tunnel, but in consequence of a difficulty which arose from the amateurish handling of the boat-hooks, so little progress was made that considerable alarm was manifested, and it is said that one vestryman followed the example of Panurge in a similar predicament, and fell on his knees and prayed fervently.   The foul air of the tunnel, the motion of the waves, or other causes, made several gentlemen extremely unwell, and two disgorged themselves involuntarily of the sandwiches of which they had liberally partaken at an earlier part of the voyage.   At length the Regent's Park end of the tunnel appeared in sight, and when the barge emerged it was found, on calling over the roll that nothing had been lost, save one vestryman who was subsequently discovered under one of the seats."

Through London by Canal – Harper's New Monthly Magazine – Vol.70, No.420, New York, May 1885, p.870

The author is travelling on a boat along the Regent's Canal.   The boat has moored alongside the towing path at the mouth of Islington tunnel with several other boats waiting for the tug to tow them through:

"It is five o'clock, out of the mouth of the tunnel come in dramatic procession two monkey-boats lashed together   . . .pushed by the tug, which tows in turn a long line of barges behind.   It is a queer sort of boat – a very broad-bottomed barge, almost the width of the tunnel; from its flat deck rises an arched iron structure nearly filling the interior of the vault.   Within this iron roof is the machinery – an engine with a drum and cog-wheels, over which is wound the chain, lying along the bed of the canal within the tunnel, by which the tug is dragged along.   The line of the tunnel is perfectly straight, 2910 feet in length, 19 feet 6 inches high, 17 feet 6 inches wide, and it is cut through the blue, the genuine London clay.   . . .The air we breathe is almost as poisonous as the delectable compound called by that name provided for the passengers by the underground railway.   . . .We are passing, here and there, streaks of water trickling down the vault in a ghastly sort of fashion; they come from the New River, which passes over the tunnel just under the crest of the hill.   We follow it in thought to where, a little further down the Islington slope, it forms its reservoir, the New River Head, which furnishes more than a quarter of the whole London water supply."

The Coming of the Railways

When Charles Dickens, as a boy of eleven, moved to London the Regent's Canal had been open and operating for more than two years; Dickens therefore took the canals for granted and barely mentions them in his writings.   The first railway reached London ten year later and ploughed through the Camden he had known as a school-boy and this stirred him to write vehemently on the subject:

Dombey and Son, by Charles Dickens, Chapter 6; 1848

"The first shock of a great earthquake had, just at that period, rent the whole neighbourhood to its centre.   Traces of its course were visible on every side.   Houses were knocked down, streets broken through and stopped; deep pits and trenches dug in the ground; enormous heaps of earth and clay thrown up; buildings that were

St. Pancras Station 1877 showing entrances at upper platform level
(Old & New London)

undermined and shaking, propped by great beams of wood. Here, a great chaos of carts, overthrown and jumbled together, lay topsy-turvy at the bottom of a steep unnatural hill; there, confused treasures of iron soaked and rusted in something that had accidentally become a pond. Everywhere were bridges that led nowhere; thoroughfares that were wholly impassable; Babel towers of chimneys, wanting half their height; temporary wooden houses and enclosures, in the most unlikely situations; carcases of ragged tenements, and fragments of unfinished walls and arches, and piles of scaffolding, and wildernesses of bricks, and giant forms of cranes, and tripods straddling above nothing. There were a hundred thousand shapes and substances of incompleteness, wildly mingled out of their places, upside down, burrowing in the earth, aspiring in the air, mouldering in the water, and unintelligible as any dream. Hot springs and fiery eruptions, the usual attendants upon earthquakes, lent their contributions of confusion to the scene. Boiling water hissed and heaved within dilapidated walls; whence, also, the glare and roar of flames came issuing forth; and mounds of ashes blocked up rights of way, and wholly changed the law and custom of the neighbourhood.

In short, the yet unfinished and unopened Railroad was in progress; and, from the very core of all this dire disorder, trailed smoothly away, upon its mighty course of civilisation and improvement."

A report on the construction of the railway into St Pancras was more philosophical:

Old and New London, Volume V, by Edward Walford, c1877, p.340

"We may add, in concluding this chapter, that the descration of the St Pancras churchyard, of which we have spoken above, was as nothing compared to the demolition of the hundreds of houses of the poorer working classes in Agar Town and Somers Town, occasioned by the extension of the Midland Railway. The extent of this clean sweep was, and is still, comparatively unknown, and has caused a very considerable portion of St Pancras parish to be effaced from the map of London. Perhaps no part of London or its neighbourhood has undergone such a rapid and extensive transformation. It will, perhaps, be said that in the long run the vicinity has benefitted in every way; but it is to be feared that in the process of improvement the weakest have been thrust rather rudely to the wall."

The railway companies wished to have their main passenger stations on the New Road which meant that the lines had to cross the Regent's Canal which lay just to the north of it. The line into Euston crossed over the canal and then had to run down a slope into the station, the early locomotives had difficulty in pulling the carriages up the incline (see page 15):

Old and New London, Vol. V, by Edward Walford, c1877, p.350

"It will be remembered that, when in 1831–2 the London and Birmingham Railway (as this line was originally called) was first projected, the metropolitan terminus was at Chalk Farm, near the north east corner of Regent's Park. It was not until 1835 that a bill was brought into Parliament, and carried after great opposition, for bringing this terminus as near to London as what was then termed 'Euston Grove'. Up to the year 1845, for fear of frightening the horses in the streets, the locomotive engines came no nearer to London than Chalk Farm, where the engine was detached from the train, and from thence to Euston Station the carriages were attached to an endless rope moved by a stationary engine at the Chalk Farm end of the line."

The line into St Pancras also crossed over the canal, but a slope into the station was avoided:

Old and New London, Vol. V, by Edward Walford, c1877, p.370

"It was found necessary to raise the level of the terminus about fifteen feet higher than the Euston Road, in order to secure good gradients and proper levels for some of the suburban stations. The space underneath was then utilised as a cellarage for the Burton and other ale traffic, and thus the entire station may be said, seriously as well as jestingly, to rest on a substratum of beer. The roof of part of the cellarage forms the flooring of the terminus and platform of the station, and is so constructed as to bear the immense weight of the many locomotive engines at the same time."

However the line into Kings Cross station crossed below the canal:

Old and New London, Vol. V, by Edward Walford, c1877, p.314

"The Grand Junction Canal, after leaving the Regent's Park, passes through Camden Town. It is spanned on the Chalk Farm Road by a fine bridge of cast iron. A little further to the east it crosses the Midland Railway, or rather the latter is carried under it. This work was effected by a triumph of engineering skill almost unparalleled. The waters of the canal are drained off every year for exactly seven days, in order to clear its bed; during this period so strong a force of men was put upon it that between one Saturday and the next a tunnel was dug under the canal, and bricked and roofed over before the water was sent back into its channel."

Agar Town

Extract from Deeds, quoted in The Story of Agar Town by Rev. R. Conyers Morrell; 1935. p.12

"1810. On March 31st, 1810, the Manor of Pancras, containing by estimation some 70 acres, was purchased at Garraway's Auction Rooms by William Agar Esquire, Barrister at Law, the purchase money being £8,000. In 1811, it was assessed as prebendal land at £504, against which Mr Agar appealed, the rent having been much less and reduced by land occupied by St Pancras Workhouse. In the course of his appeal, Mr Agar declared the extent of the estate as 72 acres, 3 roods, 26 perches.

Building leases were granted in 1831, when small houses began to be built."

A Suburban Connemara – Charles Dickens; Household Words, Vol.2, No.50, London, Saturday 8 March, 1851, p.564

"'How far does Agar Town extend?' I asked.
'Do you see them cinder heaps out a yonder?'
I looked down in the distance, and beheld a lofty chain of dark mountains. 'Well,' said the Dustman, 'that's where Hagar Town ends – close upon Battle Bridge. Them heaps is made o' breeze; breeze is the siftins of the dust what has been put there by the conteractor's men, arter takin' away all the wallyables as has been found.' ...

Crossing another bridge – for the Canal takes a winding course through the midst of this Eden – I stood beside the 'Good Samaritan' Public House to observe the houses which the dustman had pointed out, with the water 'a flowin' in at the back doors'. Along the Canalside, the huts of the settlers, of many shapes and sizes, were closely ranged. Every tenant, having, as I was informed, his own lease of the ground, appeared to have disclaimed to imitate his neighbour and to have constructed his abode according to his own ideas of beauty or convenience. There were the dog-kennel, the cow-shed, the shanty, the elongated watch-box, styles, of architecture. To another, the ingenious residence of Robinson Crusoe seemed to have given his idea. Through an opening was to be seen another layer of dwellings, at the back: one looked like a dismantled windmill; and another, perched upon a wall, like a guards look out on the top of a railway carriage. The love of variety was, everywhere, carried to the utmost pitch of extravagence. Every garden had its nuisance – so far the inhabitants were agreed – but, every nuisance was of a distinct and peculiar character. In one was a dung heap; in the next, a cinder heap; in the third which belonged to the cottage of a costermonger, were a pile of whelk and periwhinkle shells, some rotten cabbages and a donkey, and in the garden of another, exhibiting a board with the words 'Ladies School', had become a pond of thick green water, which was carefully dammed up, and prevented from flowing over upon the Canal towing path by a brick parapet."

The Midland Railway: Its Rise and Progress. A Narrative of Modern Enterprise by Frederick S. Williams; 1878. London: Strahan & Co. p.332

"Old St Pancras Churchyard was invaded, and Agar Town was almost demolished.   Yet those who knew that district at that time have no regret at the change. Time was when here the wealthy owner of a large estate had lived in his mansion; but after his departure the place became a very 'abomination of desolation.'   In its centre was what was named La Belle Isle, a dreary and unsavoury locality, abandoned to mountains of refuse from the Metropolitan dust-bins, strewn with decaying vegetables and foul-smelling fragments of what had once been fish, or occupied by knackers' yards and manure-making, bone-boiling, and soap-manufacturing works, and smoke-belching potteries and brick-kilns.   At the broken windows and doors of mutilated houses canaries still sang and dogs still lay sleeping in the sun, to remind one of the vast colonies of bird and dog-fanciers who formerly made Agar Town their abode; and from these dwellings wretched creatures came, in rags and dirt, and searched amid the far-extending refuse for the filthy treasure by the aid of which they eked out a miserable livelihood, while over the whole neighbourhood the gasworks poured forth their mephitic vapours, and the canal gave forth its rheumatic dampness, extracting in return some of the more poisonous ingredients from the atmosphere, and spreading them upon the surface of the water in a thick scum of various and ominous hues. Such was Agar Town before the Midland came."

THE REGENT'S CANAL AND ITS RELATIONSHIP TO LONDON'S WATERWAYS

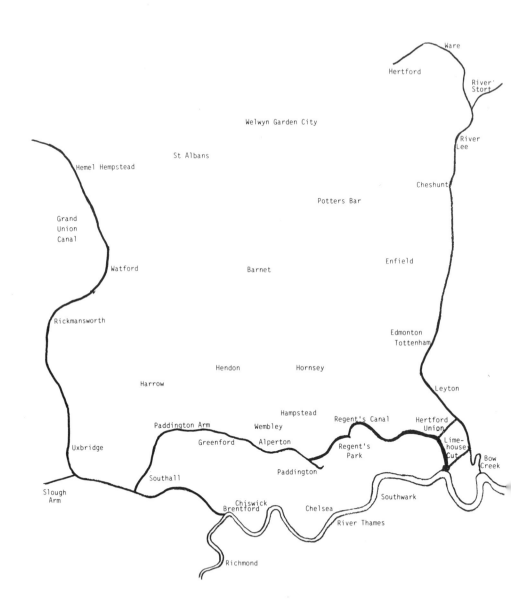

EXPLORING THE REGENT'S CANAL

The description of the Regent's Canal is intended primarily for those walking along its towing path and following the routes over the two tunnels — neither of which has a towing path through it. When indicating features on either side of the canal, it is assumed that the walker is travelling from the direction of Paddington towards Lime-house; the towing path is constantly on the left-hand side throughout the entire canal, except that it crosses the canal to pass on the right of Hampstead Road Top Lock and east of Islington Tunnel, as far as Frog Lane Bridge, the towing path itself is closed as Islington Council has provided an attractive canalside walk along the right bank. When describing buildings around a basin, the viewpoint is always taken to be from the main line of the canal.

Although the Regent's Canal passes through some fascinating parts of London, I have restricted my descriptions to the buildings and areas immediately adjacent to the waterside or which can be seen from the towing path, unless they have a direct relevance to the canal. However an exception has been made of features which occur above the line of the canal when it cuts through a tunnel.

The maps include details shown on the 25" to the mile Ordnance Survey maps of the 1890s so that changes since then become apparent. They are not drawn to scale but are thought to be helpful to the walker seeking to discover features on the canal. The Fire Insurance maps of Chas. E. Goad for 1891 were also consulted; these include details not only of the firms occupying the premises along the canal but the structure of the buildings and their contents. This gave interesting information on the businesses alongside the water. I have shown points of access to the towing path from the roads and nearby underground stations.

A great deal of development is taking place along the canal, and particularly in Limehouse Basin; I have described things as they appear at the beginning of 1987 in the hope that much of historical interest will remain. A lot of what is seen relates to the history of the canal and the reader is referred to those parts in the Brief History which forms the first part of this booklet.

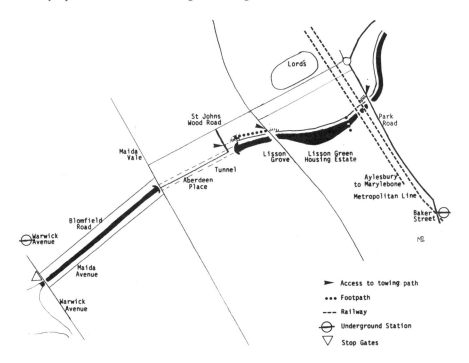

Stand in Warwick Avenue on the bridge over the canal, looking westwards towards Brownings pool with the island in its centre. Below us was the junction of the Regent's Canal with the Grand Junction Canal until amalgamation of these and other canals to form the Grand Union Canal in 1929. On the left is Rembrandt Gardens, where there are public toilets, and beyond can be seen the entrance to Paddington Basin, the terminal of the Grand Junction Canal. Ahead of us, through the bridge under Westbourne Terrace Road, stands the Canal Office; this was the toll house where dues were collected from boats setting off towards the Midlands on the Grand Junction Canal. Along the left side of the pool is the landing stage for the Zoo bus which runs from Little Venice to Camden, calling at the Zoo. Another cruise along the Regent's Canal to Camden and back is provided on Jason which leaves from Blomfield Road on the other side of Westbourne Terrace Road. Other features to be seen at Little Venice include Lady Rose of Regent, the hospitality boat owned by British Waterways Board, which is usually moored on the right hand side, adjacent to Westbourne Terrace Road, and the Cascade Art Gallery in which Alex Prowse has an exhibition of his canal paintings, reached by the gate in Blomfield Road.

Cross Warwick Avenue to see the start of the Regent's Canal. Immediately on our left is Junction House, which used to be the Regent's Canal Toll House. Every canal levied a charge based on the weight of the loads carried; this was estimated by 'gauging' a boat to determine its depth in the water, fore and aft. At the start of the Regent's Canal, under Warwick Avenue Bridge, is a pair of stop gates. Originally they were installed to prevent the Regent's Canal taking any of the Grand Junction Canal

Company's water, as required by the 1812 Act (see page 9). Their presence was recorded by John Hassell in 1819 when, referring to the 'Prince Regent's Canal' he writes "This ramification . . .commences with a lock at the first bridge" (see page 22). They are used today to isolate parts of the canal should a breach occur, or if a section needs to be drained for maintenance.

The stretch of the canal up to Maida Hill tunnel is flanked on both sides with roads lined with elegant houses, Maida Avenue on the right and Blomfield Road on the left. In Maida Avenue, about half-way along on the corner of Park Place Villas, is a house which once belonged to Lillie Langtry (1853–1929), one of the first English society women to become an actress. Other people who have been associated with the area, past or present, include Lady Diana Duff Cooper, John Julius Norwich, the author, Joan Collins, Peter Palumbo who became prominent in connection with a development plan for the City, and Ringo Starr. The towing path was along on the left but it is now used as access to the private moorings; at the approach to the tunnel the path can be seen to rise up to road level so that the horse could be led over the top. Here the canal walls seem to be supported by iron girders which cross the canal high above the water. There was once a plan to build a restaurant over the canal here, beside Maida Vale, but nothing came of it. There is no towing path through this, or any other tunnel on the Grand Union Canal, and throughout the age of the horse-drawn barge, boats had to be propelled through this tunnel by the boatmen – unlike Islington Tunnel which introduced a steam tug in 1826 (see page 27). The usual way was for the barge to be 'legged' through (see page 26). An alternative method – seen in a 1924 film entitled "Barging through London" – was for the boatman to push a pole against the roof and then walk the length of his barge. This was practical, of course, only when he had a firm, level load on board.

Maida Hill tunnel is 272 yards (250 metres) long and 16' 9" wide. The water is about 4 feet deep and the height of the roof above water level is about 10 feet. The length in metres is mentioned because these distances are marked in white paint, in ten metre lengths, along the inside of both Maida Hill and Islington tunnels. Like the horse, we have to walk over the top. Cross Maida Avenue to the zebra crossing over Maida Vale and walk up Aberdeen Place which lies immediately on top of the tunnel. Near the end, on the right, is a large red brick building, St John's Wood Electricity Station. The Central Electricity Generating Board recently laid a 400 kilo-Volt cable under the canal towing path between here and the Hertford Union Canal, carrying power from generating stations on the Thames Estuary. Almost immediately ahead is a gate leading to some wooden steps down to the towing path alongside the eastern portal of Maida Hill Tunnel.

On the opposite bank the St Marylebone Stone Yard once occupied the upper level and a travelling crane transferred stone from barges moored at the wharf below. The wharf has now been converted for a youth club making a very attractive area and often moored alongside is the narrow boat "Victoria", donated by Marks and Spencer in 1985 during the celebrations to mark the 400th anniversary of the City of Westminster, an occasion recorded on the side of the craft. On both sides of the canal the new blocks of flats have been built with views of the water, and many examples of this enlightened planning will be seen along the canal. The railings above the towing path, on the left, border a footpath in front of flats. The horse had to continue at the high level beyond the tunnel, cross Lisson Grove to return to the towing path down a sloping, cobbled path on the other side of the next bridge and then return to the tunnel mouth to pick up the towing rope.

The towing path passes under Lisson Grove and also a house on the main road — number 120 — which makes a wide bridge; a handrail has been added since the days of horse towing because the roof, high enough for a horse, is a bit low for pedestrians. The horse slope from Lisson Grove can be seen joining the towing path just beyond the hut. Here the canal opens out widely and there were moorings for commerical barges on the right-hand side adjacent to the Marylebone railway freight yards where goods were transhipped between rail and canal. When the goods yards were no longer needed, the Lisson Green Housing Estate was built by Westminster City Council. Turn and look back at the house straddling the canal. It is sometimes described as "the upside-down house"; the reason for this is that the road is at the level of the upper floor of the house so the inhabitants have to go down-stairs to bed.

On the towing path side are moorings for private non-residential boats, and it will be apparent that a vast range of types of boat may be met on the canals. There are fibre-glass cruisers, clinker-built boats — some of them seeming to be converted fishing boats — the occasional sailing boat and narrow boats, with both timber and steel hulls. Most of the steel narrow boats on the canals are newly built, not converted working narrow boats. They have a traditional hull but the interiors are often very luxurious, with gas ovens, refrigerators, running hot and cold water and, usually, a shower bath, gas or coke fires, comfortable beds and plenty of cupboards. As the public is allowed to walk alongside these moorings, it is polite to respect the privacy of their owners.

The moorings are protected by gates at either end, though these are unlocked when the canal towing path is open. Just beyond the moorings is a metal bridge over the canal from the Lisson Grove Housing Estate. This provides a good view of the sweep of the canal as far as Lisson Grove. Behind the wall alongside the towing path, is the sign "Thames Bank Iron Company". This once had a branch line from the Great Central Line; the course of the curved track round the wall can be seen. The new white buildings behind the curved wall belongs to IBM.

Walk along the towing path under three bridges. The first is the line into Marylebone Station; it used to be the Great Central Line from London to Manchester, Nottingham and Sheffield, but now provides a commuter service between London and Aylesbury and Banbury. There were proposals to close this line and plans were considered for a coach terminal at Marylebone Station so that coaches could take advantage of an exclusive route along the old course into London. However British Rail has recently announced that the line has been reprieved as there are doubts on whether the passenger traffic could be absorbed by the underground system. The second bridge carries the Metropolitan Line from Baker Street to Watford and Amersham while the third bridge, recorded on 'old maps as Chapel Bridge, is Park Road; steps lead up from the towing path to a gate giving access to this road. Close by is Lord's Cricket Ground, the siting of which was affected by the building of the Regent's Canal and its surface was levelled with spoil from Maida Hill Tunnel (see page 8).

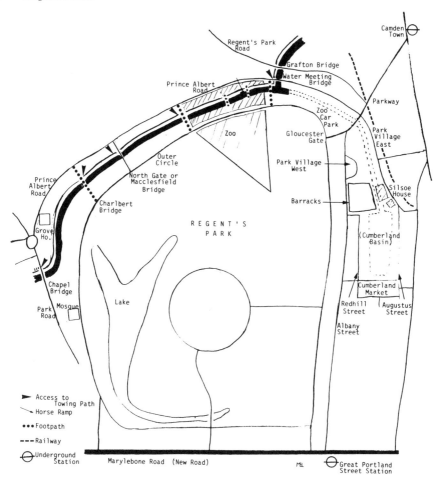

Just beyond Park Road bridge the canal swings north as it enters Regent's Park; it is now in a deep cutting, some twenty-five feet deep, which effectively hides it from the neighbourhood. This excavation would have been avoided had the canal taken a more southerly route through the centre of the Park as originally planned (see page 4). It is possible to see, through the trees on the right, the minaret — and sometimes the dome — of the Central Islamic Mosque in Regent's Park.

Regent's Park was laid out by John Nash and his assistant, James Morgan between 1810 and 1838. Residential accommodation in the park consisted of elegant terraces around it and private villas within it; these were largely the work of two architects, John Nash and James Burton, both of whom had considerable investment in the estate. They were keen to attract wealthy, cultivated tenants for their properties; one such gentleman was George Greenough who approached James Burton with a view to taking a lease on a villa in the park. Burton and Nash were too busy to undertake a new project but suggested that Burton's son, Decimus, should be the architect. Decimus Burton had served six years, mainly in his father's office, and this was to be his first important commission. The site chosen was three acres in the strip of land isolated from the park by the Regent's Canal, and here he built Grove House in 1822–24. It can be seen on the left of the towing path in the well-kept grounds just inside the Park. Subsequently the occupants of Grove House, or Grove Lodge as it was sometimes called, have included Frank Smedley, the writer, Thomas Greer, M.P. who in 1877 had the house enlarged, and Sigismund Goetze, the artist. It was then leased by the Midland Bank Ltd. for the use of its Chairman and in 1953 it became the Headquarters of the Nuffield Foundation, and its name was changed to Nuffield Lodge. The gardens are under the management of the botanical research department of University College, London (8). The Nuffield Foundation has recently vacated the property, and it has been bought for a private residence.

Beyond Nuffield Lodge can be seen the blocks of flats along Prince Albert Road. The first bridge in the park is an unusual structure; it looks very sturdy and it is surprising, when people walk across it, to see that there is only a footpath on top of it. This is the aqueduct which carries the River Tyburn over the Canal. The Tyburn, now entirely underground, rises on Haverstock Hill and runs south west to Prince Albert Road, crossing the canal to enter the grounds of the residence of the American Ambassador. It then flows into the lake in Regent's Park and continues down as far as Buckingham Palace. Here it divides, and two branches flow into the Thames on either side of the Houses of Parliament and Westminster Abbey forming an island — Thorney Island — on which the Palace of Westminster was built.

The next bridge was designed in 1829 by James Elmes; its elegant arches are supported on five pairs of cast-iron columns bearing the name "Coalbrookdale" on their capitals. This bridge has three names; it was called Macclesfield Bridge after the first Chairman of the Regent's Canal Company, the Earl of Macclesfield, and it is also known as North Gate Bridge as it is the only road entrance to the Park on its north side and used to have gates between the bridge and Prince Albert Road. Its third name is "Blow-up Bridge" following the disaster on 2 October, 1874, when a barge of blasting gunpowder exploded and demolished it (see page 15). When the bridge was rebuilt the cast-iron columns were used again but as the two end columns on the towing path side had grooves worn in them by the ropes used by horses towing barges the columns were erected the other way round in order to provide an un-damaged surface for the ropes. Examination of the end columns will reveal the grooves on the side away from the canal; had a horse attempted to pass on this side it would have pulled the barge out of the water. These grooves were therefore worn in the first forty-five years of the life of the bridge and the grooves on the canal side were worn after the bridge had been rebuilt. On the bank on the approach to the bridge on the towing path side will be seen a plane tree which survived the explosion over a century ago and still bears the scars.

The significance of Coalbrookdale on the column tops is that the Shropshire town was the site of the world's first coke-fired blast furnace, built by Abraham Darby in 1709, (24) and regarded by many as the birthplace of the industrial revolution. Certainly the ability to cast large iron structures in place of the pots and pans which represented the limits of charcoal fired iron smelting made possible the production of heavy machinery. This in turn led to demands for better transport not only for the goods manufactured in factories but of the fuel needed by them. The columns were most probably delivered here by water, either through the inland waterways of the country or round the coast; there was a choice of inland routes open by 1829.

Continue along the towing path to the footbridge over the Canal. This (like the next two bridges) is a delicate structure – unlike the sturdy mass of the Tyburn Aqueduct – and it marks the beginning of the Zoo; laid out by Decimus Burton in 1827, the zoo now occupies some 36 acres and is said to house some 8,000 species of animals, birds, reptiles and fish(25). On the right a variety of quadrupeds and members of the public can be seen lining the terraces; on the left, overhanging the towing path, is the impressive aviary designed by Lord Snowdon and opened in 1965. Although boats are allowed to tie up practically anywhere on the canal system, they may not do so on this stretch through the zoo. A lot of passenger carrying boats use this Canal, such as the Zoo bus run by the London Waterbus Company between Camden and Little Venice, the Jenny Wren and the Fair Lady cruising Restaurant operated by Jenny Wren Cruises from Camden, and Jason's cruises from Blomfield Terrace, Paddington. Moored boats could cause some obstruction to this traffic; furthermore, boaters might slip into the zoo by the back door without paying.

A zoo footbridge crosses the canal near the aviary. Just past the bridge, on the right bank, is the landing stage for the zoo used by the London Waterbus Company; composite tickets which include entry to the zoo may be bought on the bus. Opposite the landing stage, beside the towing path, are two upright stones, one marked 'S M B 1821' (St Mary le Bone) and the other 'St P.P. 1842' (St Pancras Parish), being the old Parish boundary marks. Another boundary stone can be seen on the bank across the canal. There is a second footbridge linking two sections of the zoo on either side of the Canal – with a horse ramp in the towing path near it – and a further footbridge, dated 1864, marking the end of the zoo. Beneath it are two metal plates marking the boundary between the City of Westminster and the London Borough of Camden and above the water is a warning notice to boaters "DEAD SLOW – SHARP BEND AHEAD", a further consequence of the decision to route the canal around the northern perimeter of Regent's Park instead of through it as intended originally; a brick wall and a small pumping station on the right is where the canal would have emerged from the park towards Camden (see page 4). Ahead of us is the remains of the Cumberland Arm, now commonly called Cumberland Basin, with the Gallery Boat Chinese Restaurant on the left bank of it.

This arm used to continue three quarters of a mile round the eastern side of the Park to the Cumberland Basin serving a meat, vegetable and hay market close to the 'New Road' near Euston Station.   In 1948 the Basin and part of the arm were filled in with London's bomb rubble.   To explore this abandoned arm, go up the slope on the left of the towing path to Prince Albert Road; the first turning on the left is a footbridge over the canal leading to the Outer Circle in the Park.   Turn left to the zoo car and coach park — constructed on the infilled Cumberland Arm; it is worth walking to the end of the car park and onto the grass to the Parkway Bridge, now bricked up underneath.   It is a cast iron bridge with a span of fifty-three feet, surmounted with elaborate ornaments at each end — one of them is now missing.   There are some carvings of faces and still life studies in the stonework below road level on either side of the bridge.

Return to the Outer Circle of the Park and turn left through Gloucester Gate into Parkway.   On the right-hand side, at the top of Albany Road, is a plaque which informs us:

Vestry of St. Pancras
Gloucester Gate Bridge and Approach Road
This Bridge and Approach Road
was
opened for public traffic on the 3rd Day of August 1878 by
Field Marshal H R H the Duke of Cambridge

This replaced an earlier bridge, described by Walford in his 'Old and New London' in 1877: "It may be mentioned here that the bridge over the Regent's Canal between the 'York and Albany' and Gloucester Gate, having been long considered too narrow and ill-constructed to suit the requirements of the present day, the Metropolitan Board of Works have decided upon rebuilding it upon a much larger scale, at an estimated cost of about £20,000.   It will form a very handsome approach and entrance to the Regent's Park on the Eastern side." (7d)

Notice the decorative theme, including roses, on the stonework which has been continued in the ironwork of the bridge.   From the bridge the old course — now dry — can be seen between the ends of the gardens in Albany Road and Park Village East, and it is possible to get a glimpse of it from Park Village West, a crescent off Albany Street.   It is more interesting to walk down Park Village East, which curves to follow the line of the Cumberland Arm — with the railway into Euston on the left-hand side of the road.   Opposite the end of Mornington Street there is a railing which gives a good view of the width of the canal at this point.

Just beyond here is a new block of flats, Silsoe House, which has been built right across the old course.   Walk past the flats and turn right into the entrance to their car ports under the building.   In front of us is the rear of the barracks in Albany Street.   To the right — that is behind Silsoe House — the walls of the barracks are now built on the edge of the wharf which used to serve them.   In the early Nash plans of Regent's Park the barracks are shown on the north side of the park with the canal initially running in front (see page 5), then by the back of them.   They were certainly built on their present site soon after the canal opened; Joseph Priestley recorded in 1831.   ". . . a branch runs southwards to Cumberland Market, where there is a basin, passing in its course the Horse Barracks and the Jew's Harp." (26)

Facing the back of the barracks, look to the left; it is apparent that the canal widened out here. Walk past the back of Richmond House and ahead of us we see the expanse of Cumberland Basin with the grand building at the far end crowned with a clock tower. On the left were, at the turn of the century, an aerated water manufactory and a vinegar works, with timber yards on the right. At the end, on the right of the clock tower, was a piano factory. The filled-in basin is now used for allotments. Continue down Augustus Street to Cumberland Market and turn to face the elegant main entrance to the basin with its wrought iron gates.

Cumberland Basin

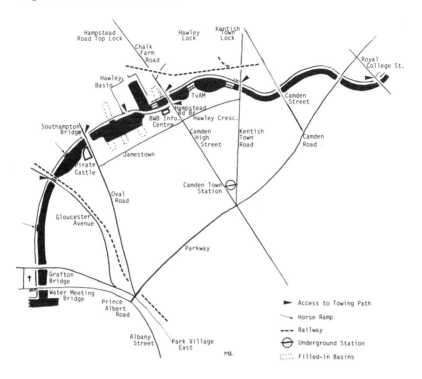

Where the Canal leaves Regent's Park, it turns sharp left to pass under Prince Albert Road by 'Water Meeting Bridge' re-built in 1969. On the left is St Mark's Church. The next bridge, under Regent's Park Road, is Grafton Bridge. Seen from the canal, the brickwork is as built in 1816; the bridge has had to be strengthened to carry modern traffic and this has been done by building a new bridge within the structure of the old so that the original facing has been left intact. On the right are some elegant houses, one with Victorian cast-iron balconies and next to this is a garden containing a number of statues and a bust of Lloyd George. People associated with this area, recent and present, include Clive Jenkins, the General Secretary of the Association of Scientific, Technical, and Managerial Staffs, A.J.P. Taylor, the Oxford don and historian, and Lord St Davids, who started the Pirate's Club in 1966 and is now a leading campaigner for boats to be driven by electric power to reduce pollution on the canals — his own electrically powered boat, Silver Sail, is usually moored along here.

Notice the horse-ramp by the towing path; the cobbled slope is fairly intact, but better examples can be seen further along the canal. This stretch has recently become a **BWB** short-stay mooring and there are often visiting boats from other parts of the country tied up here. If the owners are seen to be not too busy, they will not usually object to being spoken to and may be pleased to tell you about their journey to London and about their boat. Most boaters on the canals are enthusiasts and those who do not own their own craft frequently hire boats year after year so that they may

Grooves worn by ropes in ironwork —
oblique footbridge over Hampstead Road Locks

explore the system and enjoy the tranquillity of cruising through Britain.

We reach a cluster of bridges across the canal; the first is Gloucester Avenue, with steps up to the road from the towing path. At one time a painted notice stood under this bridge on the right-hand side proclaiming: "You are about to be raided by pirates — have your treasure ready". The Pirate Club urgently needed funds to provide adequate accommodation. At the time the Club was using a barge moored beyond the bridges, canoes dangling from its sides, and the young members would approach people using the canal seeking contributions. It was all very good-humoured and passengers on trip boats, such as the Zoo Bus, Jason's Cruise and Jenny Wren, and boat owners were happy to make a donation. The other bridges carry the main railway line into Euston Station. The abutments of the original 1837 bridge, built by Robert Stephenson, may be seen under the further bridge. Just beyond them, on the left high over the towing path, once stood the stationary steam engine which used to lower the carriages by wire cables down the slope into Euston Station and then haul them up again when the train was ready to depart (see page 15). When no longer needed the steam engine was exported to Russia. There is a horse ramp on the other side of this bridge, ramps will be found on either side of every railway bridge along the canal.

Often moored on the right of the canal is the "Pirate Princess", a narrow boat built for the Rainbow Trust by shipyard apprentices and handed over by Prince Charles on 2 June, 1982. The Pirate Club is, for most of the time, a hive of activity with canoists paddling about the water. It has provided children with the opportunity of getting familiar with the water and thus being safer on it. Despite the fact that this is a busy waterway with trip boats and private craft moving along the canal, I have never seen any incident invloving a boat and a canoe; those in canoes keep a wary eye on the traffic and they are very well behaved, a credit to the Club. On the opposite bank was once one of the several properties in the area of Messrs W & A Gilbey, the gin distillers and wine merchants. A railway line crossed the canal to it immediately adjacent to the next bridge, Southampton Bridge; evidence of the railway bridge can be seen in the wall of the castle. The Pirate Castle was built by Richard Siefert & Partners for the Pirate Club and opened in 1977. On the towing path side, on the left of the Pirate Castle, is a pumping station built in 1980 by the Central Electricity Generating Board. It circulates water around the cables to keep them cool and several such pumps have been provided along the towing path. The feature of this one is that the C.E.G.B. has taken the trouble to reproduce the style of the Castle so the total effect, including the footbridge and the portcullis beneath it, is very impressive.

Steps by the CEGB pumping station lead to Oval Road which crosses the canal to a large storage warehouse. Gilbey used to occupy the large white building on the right beyond the bridge as well as the brick building on the left. The towing path rises here to cross over the entrance to a basin beneath the large red brick warehouse into which railway lines ran at ground level. This was a canal/railway interchange warehouse and the basin led to a vast network of underground vaults — the Camden Catecombs once used for the storage of wines and spirits — through what was sometimes known as Dead Dog Tunnel. Work has started on restoring this warehouse, possibly as an extension to Camden market. Notice the grooves worn by ropes in the iron and stonework on the canal side of the towing path. The canal is wider here and on the opposite side there used to be entrances to further basins, two near the white Gilbey building and a third near the end of the oblique iron bridge; they are now filled in.

Before crossing the oblique bridge, turn left through the doorway leading to Dingwalls Timber Wharf and Dock Basin; in 1973 this was opened as the Camden Lock Centre with craft shops and artists' workshops in the converted stables and hay lofts. Camden market is very lively at weekends, with stalls offering a wide variety of goods and refreshments, and with musicians and performers entertaining the crowds. It is from here that the London Waterbus leaves for the zoo and Little Venice. There are toilets on the right-hand side of the basin.

Cross the oblique bridge which has a span of eighty feet to take the towing path across to the right-hand side of the locks; notice the cobble stones to give the horse a grip and look at the handrail on the right-hand side. In it you will see deep grooves worn by the ropes as the horses pulled the barges out of the locks. All along the canal we can see the evidence of the working of commercial craft in the heyday of the canal. This bridge is said to be a classical example of tension and compression mechanics; a plaque on the right support under the bridge explains the details. Standing near the foot of the bridge is a winch which is now preserved; it was moved here when no longer required for opening lock gates at the Limehouse Barge Lock which was abandoned in 1968 (see page 68). On the right used to be stables — this was one of the three places where boatmen would change horses between Paddington and Limehouse.

We are now at Hampstead Road Top Lock, the first of twelve locks on the Regent's Canal which drops the level some eighty-six feet down to Limehouse Basin (Limehouse Basin is semi-tidal so the exact drop depends on the height of the tide — see page 66). Like all the locks on the Regent's Canal, this was built as a double lock. Notice the column bearing a rack and pinion on the centre island between the locks.

This used to operate the paddle which allowed water to flow from one lock to the other to conserve water (see page 9). The paddle gear for the locks themselves is of the conventional Grand Junction Canal type. The white lock cottage on the right of the locks, originally built in 1815 and enlarged in 1972, was converted in 1985/6 as a Regent's Canal Information Centre. Here BWB staff can provide a wealth of information on the canal and there is an exhibition of pictures illustrating scenes from its history.

We must now cross the canal again, like the horse, by leaving the gate on the right of the lock and walking over the bridge. Although the lock is called Hampstead Road Lock the road is, of course, no longer Hampstead Road but Chalk Farm Road; as we will see all along the canal, names known by boatmen have remained unchanged even though the names of local roads and buildings may have changed. On the opposite side of the road is the office of Jenny Wren Cruises which has access to the canal with its own landing stage. Once over the bridge turn sharp right into the first gate and walk down the slope to the towing path. On the right of the slope, in the space now occupied by Dingwalls Market, was another basin. The original bridge was built in brick in 1815 but it was replaced in 1876 by the present iron bridge; the keystone of the original bridge is set in the brickwork on the left near the bottom of the slope. At the corner of the bridge by the towing path is a vertical iron roller which prevented the ropes from cutting grooves in the stonework.

Under the bridge at the far end are the names of Parish Officers who used to be concerned with roads and bridges. Ahead of us can be seen two further locks and the pounds between them are widened in order to provide sufficient water to fill the lock chambers without an appreciable drop in the water level in the pounds. On the other side of the canal is the mooring for Jenny Wren and the Fair Lady Cruising Restaurant, and beyond it is a brightly decorated building with a row of boiled eggs in their egg-cups on the roof. Originally Camden Brewery Co Ltd., this was until fairly recently Henley's warehouse which was taken over by TV—AM, the breakfast television company for its studios. In the conversion the walls alongside the canal were retained but the rest of the building was rebuilt to provide two studios and other television facilities with a staff canteen overlooking the water. Here is Hawley lock and in common with the remaining locks down to Limehouse, the second chamber was recently converted into a weir. Notice the hydraulic paddle gear on the lower gates (see page 20); the central paddle on the island between the two locks has been removed on this and all other locks except two. The railway seen on a viaduct running alongside the canal on the left was once the East and West India Dock and Birmingham Junction Railway; it is now a branch of the north London line going to Primrose Hill. The North London line itself from Richmond ran, until recently, into Broad Street but now continues to North Woolwich via Stratford in East London; its viaduct is beyond the Primrose Hill branch and the junction is at Camden Road.

The next lock is Kentish Town Lock and beside it on the left was once a pumping station which pumped water back past the "Hampstead Road 3", as they were called by boatmen (27), to above Hampstead Road Top Lock (see page 11). On the far side of the lock are some old warehouses recently repaired and converted into a theatre scenery painting shop. The white bridge is Kentish Town Road and there is access to the canal by steps on the left. Just beyond the bridge on the right of the canal was a large building entirely faced with white tiles; the Aerated Bread Company building, with its own wharfs and cranes for unloading barges; it has recently been demolished, to be replaced by a Sainsbury's hyper-market. Beside the towing path is a vertical red post; this was another roller to protect the brickwork from the ropes hauled by horses towing barges, the rotation must have jammed when it was in use because the surface of the roller is deeply grooved. The next bridge is Camden Street, on a bend in the towing path. Notice the iron guards, to protect the brickwork on the corners of this bridge, in which ropes have worn very deep grooves, wet ropes pick up grit which makes them very abrasive. The handrail between the towing path and the canal is a recent innovation. The bridge has been extended to provide a forecourt for a garage above the canal.

The canal swings right here and beneath the corner runs the River Fleet in a culvert. When Charles Dickens left Chatham as a boy of ten in December, 1822, he came to live at 16, Bayham Street, close by the canal, with the River Fleet running down the other side of the road. The house was demolished in 1910 to make way for the Outpatients' Department of Hampstead General and North West London Hospital, built in 1912 and is still owned by a health authority. Camden Road bridge is fairly wide and the structure underneath it suggests that at one time there were two brick bridges beside each other which were subsequently joined together with iron joists. I can find no evidence on old maps that this was the case.

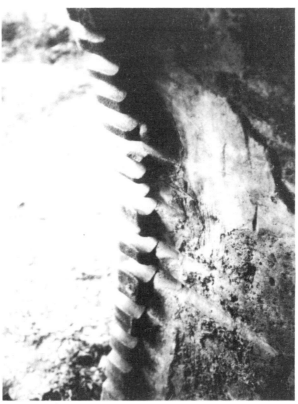

Grooves worn by ropes in ironwork —
iron guards under Camden Street Bridge

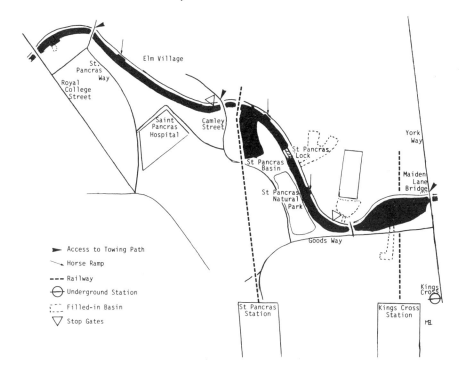

Elm Village

St.
Pancras
Way

Royal
College
Street

Saint
Pancras
Hospital

Camley
Street

York
Way

St Pancras
Lock

St Pancras
Basin

Maiden
Lane
Bridge

St Pancras
Natural
Park

Goods Way

Kings
Cross

Access to Towing Path

Horse Ramp

Railway

Underground Station

Filled-in Basin

St Pancras
Station

Kings Cross
Station

Stop Gates

Beyond the bridge on the far side Devonshire Wharf has been occupied by Lawford & Sons, builders' supplies merchants, for more than a century. On the left are the basements of the houses in Lyme Terrace. Round the corner is Royal College Street bridge. Once called Great College Street, the name refers to the Royal Veterinary College. Notice that the bridge was originally built of brick, fifteen feet wide – sufficient for a horse and cart – but that it has since been widened for local traffic. There is access to the road by steps and a slope just beyond the bridge; take a look at the width of the modern road and try to envisage what it looked like before widening. Just beyond the bridge on the right are two buildings alongside the canal; the first is now owned by HSAG, design consultants, who have provided attractive seating areas and their staff canteen beside the water and next to it is a three storey building now used by The Poster Shop.   This was once a piano factory and was restored very sympathetically during 1986. There used to be a basin to the left of it.

The St Pancras Way bridge was until recently an elaborate cast iron structure but it has been modernised. The loss of the iron panels has at least opened up the canal to the view of passers-by, a benefit which is evident at many places along the canal. The stone on the right side of the bridge records that it was opened on Thursday, March 4th, 1897.   There are steps to the road which used to be called King's Road; as it continues on the far side of the canal it drops to below the level of the water.   The canal was here built on sloping land, cut into high ground on the left and with an embankment to contain the water on the right. On the far side of St Pancras Way can

1870 – Note Railway over canal

1978 – After the fire barge sunk

Burton Warehouse 1865 – 1978

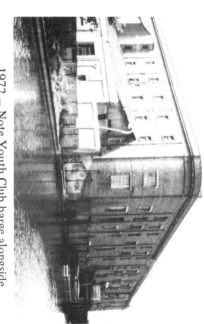

1972 – Note Youth Club barge alongside

1979 – Site cleared but railway bridge still in position

be seen the red brick building with the squre tower and arched windows which was the IDRIS factory. On the waterside used to be an organ factory and another piano factory. There is a horse ramp in the towing path.

Beyond the wall on the left side was Elm Lodge, the residence of "Councillor" Agar, who owned a considerable estate here and delayed the building of the canal by demanding substantial compensation (see page 5). In 1840 his son, William Talbot Agar, let out plots of the land to paupers and a shanty town of several hundred shacks and hovels grew up, called Agar Town, a veritable slum. Charles Dickens described it vividly in 'Household Words' in 1851 (see page 30). The town was swept away in 1868 by the Midland Railway Company for its marshalling yards but when these were no longer needed, Camden Council took it over for the Elm Village Industrial Estate and, bordering the canal, residential accommodation called 'The Village in Camden' or, as it is described on one of the two seating areas which project over the towing path, Elm Village, built in 1983. The canal is rightly called the Grand Union (see page 12).

Further along the towing path, is a modern wharf with blue steel doors and next to it is a red brick tower, over the towing path opposite the tower can be seen the base of a bridge in the wall, this once carried a railway line over to the opposite side of the canal to the Burton Warehouse, built in 1865 to house 100,000 barrels of Bass ale. The warehouse changed its function on a number of occasions and in the mid 1970s carried a faded sign proclaiming F.W. Woolworth & Co. Against it was moored a barge used by Camden Canoe Club, and it was here in September 1977 that the Mayor of Camden, Councillor Bob Humphreys, was attending an event at the Club when he fell into the canal (see page 23). Sadly the warehouse burned down in 1978 and the barge sank. The Club moved into a building on the side of the towin path and opened the Jubilee Waterside Canoe Centre. Unfortunately this burned down 1983, but it has been rebuilt and re-opened as the Jubilee Waterside Centre. The site of the Burton warehouse has now been developed by the Post Office for its Royal Mail North Western District Office. To the left of it is St Pancras Hospital and Hospital for Tropical Diseases, once an isolation hospital but now used as a wing of University College Hospital, mainly for geriatric patients. The oblique bridge, recently modernised, used to be Cambridge Street linking Agar Town to Somers Town; it is now Camley Street and there are steps up to it from the Towing path just before the bridge. The canal narrows here and there is a pair of stop gates which are closed if a section of the canal is de-watered.

The bridges beyond Camley Street, constructed at Park Gate Steel Works, Rotherham, in 1868, carry the Midland Railway into St Pancras. The lines crossed over the canal and the main line station was then built up at the same level, seventeen feet above ground level, with warehouses and shops beneath it (see page 15). There is a horse ramp close to the bridge. Just beyond, on the right, is a basin over which once ran railway sidings used by the Railway Company for the discharge of cinders from locomotives into barges — some remnants of iron girders projecting near the top of the wall mark the site of the bridge. It is now used as moorings by the St Pancras Cruising Club.

To the left of the towing path were the freight yards of the Great Northern Railway. St Pancras Lock is the only pair on the Regent's Canal at which the left-hand lock has been converted to a weir. It causes a problem for boaters because below the lock there is only a tiny landing stage for the crew to disembark to operate the locks; British Waterways Board is investigating possible solutions to the problem. The cottage is no longer needed for a lock-keeper and is on lease. Below the lock on the left, the towing path crosses an entrance to a basin serving stone and coal wharfs operated by the Great Northern Railway. The line from London to Doncaster was built in 1846 to handle coal from South Yorkshire and by 1867 it was handling nearly a million tons a year. The basin is now filled in and the entrance bricked up. Notice how the towing path over the bridge is paved with granite sets to help the horse to get a grip, the markings of a similar bridge will be seen round the next corner though that one has been completely removed.

A short distance beyond the lock a bridge used to take a railway line from the Great Northern yards on the left to coal chutes in the Camley Street Coal Depot on the right of the canal. This has now been removed but in the film "Alfie" (1966) Michael Caine is seen walking beside St Pancras Lock and the girder bridge is behind him; the row of stone blocks in the brickwork over the sixth bricked up arch near the bottom of the slope in the towing path indicate its position. There is another horse ramp near by. The coal depot on the right became a junk heap until the London Wildlife Trust and the London Borough of Camden created a wild life refuge with areas of marsh, reedbeds, meadow and woodland edge to see what wild plants, butterflies and birds will be attracted to it. The Camley Street Natural Park was opened in 1985 and an information centre has been built, with a manager appointed by the London Wildlife Trust.

Behind the Camley Street Natural Park stand the gas holders which used to form part of the Imperial Gas Works. A plaque on one of them records that it was built in 1864 and telescoped in 1880; the gas holders are still in use and are listed structures. A contemporary book reports that "the Gas Works poured forth their mephitic vapours". (see page 31). Behind the gas holders can be seen the single span of St Pancras main line station with the Midland Grand Hotel at the back, built by Gilbert Scott in 1868; the hotel closed in 1935 and was, until recently, used by British Rail for offices. Now a listed building, it may be used again as an hotel.

Along the left side of the towing path is a curving brick wall with the remnants of windows in it at ground floor level. Behind here were the railway company's stables; goods unloaded from trains were distributed in London by horse and cart. Above, on the corner, stood the company's coal offices, they were damaged by fire in 1983 and the towing path below them was closed for a considerable period until the building was made safe. On the corner was Somers Town Bridge — now demolished but the row of stone blocks in the wall above the towing path mark its position — and a railway bridge which carried coal from the Great Northern coal depot to the Imperial Gas Works; of this bridge there is now no trace. The canal narrows here and a pair of stop gates can be seen on either side. These were installed in the second world war to protect the railway tunnels under the canal a short distance away; when the air raid warning sounded, these gates, and a similar pair under Maidens Lane Bridge, were closed so that should a bomb damage the canal the amount of water flooding the railways would be limited.

The next bridge, a recent concrete structure, is a private entrance from Goods Way into the Granary, now used by national carriers. The Granary was built for the Great Northern Railway Company by Lewis Cubbitt at about the same time as he was building the main line passenger terminus at Kings Cross Station, opened in 1852. A newspaper report in 1851 tells us about the area at the time: "The Great Northern Company, in addition to their extensive coal depots at their present temporary terminus in Maiden-lane, are having constructed an immense granary. This building is situate on the southern side of the station, abutting on a spacious dock, constructed on the northern side of the Regent's Canal, and immediately facing the dock and works belonging to the Imperial Gas Company. From this dock there exists two cuttings or creeks, running into the Granary, constructed for the purpose of enabling barges to run in and receive the grain under cover of the building itself, and to facilitate the loading and unloading of goods." (28). The granary occupied the upper floors and at ground level the railway freight depot allowed goods to be transferred directly into and out of barges. The channels beneath the building communicated with a basin in front of it and this linked with the Regent's Canal through an arch which was bricked up when the basin was filled in; the position of the arch is clearly visible in the wall beside the towing path, and it will be seen that the towing path used to rise over it as it does just below St Pancras Lock. (see above). The future of this area is under discussion.

On the other side of the bridge the canal widens out. On the right of the canal, just beyond the old Goods Way Mooring, is a black wall which now blocks the old entrance to the Imperial Gas Company's coal basin. From here it used to be possible to see the single span of St Pancras Station to the right and the double span of Kings Cross Station in front of us, a new brick wall of the rebuilt petrol station has reduced this view but on climbing the bank beside the towing path it is possible to see them. The main line out of Kings Cross crosses below the canal in two tunnels, each approximately twenty feet wide, and twenty feet apart. On the wall, about four feet above the top of the bank, the word 'tunnel' has been painted in two places, thirty-five feet apart, indicating the location of a tunnel; it was probably marked by maintenance engineers undertaking work here. The Great Northern Railway was carried under the canal in 1852 when Kings Cross Station was built as the London Terminus to replace the Station in York Road, the work was done in one week during which time the Regent's Canal was closed to traffic (see page 29). The position previously occupied by the temporary station on York Road was then used for an immense potato market. The Piccadilly Line was built under the canal here in 1903.

Steps lead up from the towing path to the bridge beside a yellow brick building with a notice identifying it as Maiden Lane Pumping Station. This is another of the pumping stations provided by the CEGB to keep their cables under the towing path cool. The bridge is still known to canal users as Maiden Lane Bridge though the road is now York Way. The name is said by some to be a corruption of 'Muddy Lane' as this was Longwich Lane, the main road out of London to the north, described in 1593 by John Norden: "The old and auncient high waie to high Bernet, from Portepoole, now Grayes Inne, as also from Clerkenwell, was through a lane, on the east of Pancras Church, called Longwich Lane . . .This auncient high way, was refused of wayfaring men, and carriers, by reason of the deepness and dirtie passage in the winter season" (29). A more likely explanation for the change of name from Longwich Lane to Maiden Lane is that the road once passed through the area of the middens or refuse heaps about which Charles Dickens wrote so vividly. In fact the road has had several names including Black Dog Lane, Brecknock Road and then York Road because the London and York Railway had a temporary main line terminus here before it opened King's Cross Station and became the Great Northern Railway. It is now York Way and is the boundary between the London Boroughs of Camden and of Islington.

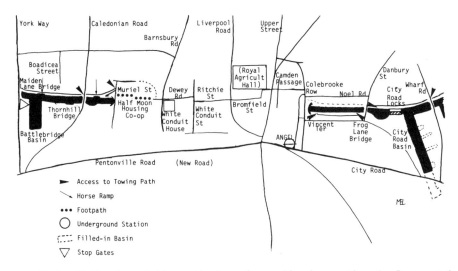

Under Maiden Lane bridge notice how the road has been widened. Just past the bridge is the second pair of stop gates closed when the air raid sirens sounded in the second world war to avoid too much flooding of the railway tunnels. The new red brick building on the right of the canal has replaced the Westinghouse Brake Company offices demolished in the 1970s; it stands on the corner of Horsfall Basin – so called because it was built on land owned by Mr Horsfall – or Battle Bridge Basin as it is now more commonly known. Battle Bridge is the old name for Kings Cross, marking, it is said, the place where Queen Boadicea attacked the Romans in AD 61, killing every one of them and burning their possessions. These Romans were, however, only a small garrison and a Roman Legion hurried back from the north, defeating her in Essex. Boadicea Street is immediately to the north of the canal at this point. Battle Bridge became King's Cross in 1830 when a statue of George VI was erected at the junction of the six roads which met there; described as a "hideous monstrosity" (30a), it was removed in 1845.

Behind the red brick building on the right of the basin is the Waterside Inn, with seating overlooking the water, and beyond this are some old warehouses, with arched windows, which now have a preservation order on them. There is no such order on the building across the bottom of the basin, bearing the notices "Jams & Marmalade" "Plaistowe & Co", which was once J Dickenson's paper warehouse, now due for demolition. On the left were timber wharfs and saw mills, a flour mill and 'ice wells' owned by Carlo Gatti, an Italian who was an ice merchant. A property in New Wharf Road has just been acquired by the Regent's Canal Group where it plans to establish a museum. This side is now used as moorings for the London Narrow Boat Association; the boat "Tarporley" owned by Camden Council's Youth Work, is frequently moored here even though it is just outside its Borough. In the towing path opposite the end of the basin there is a horse ramp. Notice also the attractive litter bins placed along the canal in Islington by the Borough Council. Riparian Councils have also placed life belts along the canal for use if anybody should fall into the water; sadly many of them reach the water as an act of vandalism rather than in an emergency.

Continuing along the canal, on the right, there is a large warehouse with entrances at each floor, served with cranes to transfer goods between barges and the storage areas. A notice reads:

DANGER
When using hoist all load must
be slung by 'slip' slings
Any loader failing to do this
will be instantly dismissed

Employees must not work
underneath a hoisted load

The wharfs were worked by James Thorley & Son; "'Thorley's Food for Cattle' stares us in the face from huge signs, and its huge works stretch along the canal" wrote a reporter in 1885 (20). It was taken over in 1957 by Charles Bartlett Co., Export Packers, which replaced the name of Thorley on the stack with its own. However on the east end of the building some of the earlier writing can be discerned; above the upper row of three windows "Thorleys" is seen and below them odd letters – an 'F' and an 'A' – can just be identified. The warehouses on the towing path side have been recently demolished and new dwellings are being built in their place. Just before the next bridge is a small public garden which gives access to Caledonian Road, which crosses the canal by Thornhill Bridge.

George Thornhill owned the land through which the canal was dug and not only is his name used for a local road, square, crescent, bridge, school and wharfs but the names of his children were remembered too; walking from Thornhill Square we pass Matilda Street, Shirley Street, Everilda Street, Edward Square, Charlotte Terrace, Muriel Street, Rodney Street and Cynthia Street, and on old maps we find Francis Street, Bryan Street and Square, William Street and Henry Square all in this area; I do not know if these were all his progeny but many of them certainly were. Thornhill bridge itself has been replaced by a modern structure to carry the Caledonian Road traffic. Further along on the right bank is Fife Terrace containing some houses built soon after the canal was opened. Those nearer the tunnel mouth were demolished to make way for newer properties. The Barnsbury Estate on the left is a recent development which won an award in the Canal Way Project for improving the environment of the canal. Notice the horse ramp.

Ahead is Islington Tunnel, 960 yards long (875 metres, marked along the right wall inside the tunnel every ten metres) and 60ft below the summit, some 17 feet wide, about 4 feet deep and with a height above the water of 9ft.9ins. The tunnel was designed by James Morgan when the competition for a tunnel design failed to produce any satisfactory results (see page 7). There is no towing path through the tunnel and initially boats had to be legged through (see page 26), and the horse was led up the slope on the left to walk over the top of the hill. A steam tug was introduced in 1826 and continued in use until the 1930s (see page 27). Although two narrow boats can pass in the tunnel, it is usual in a short tunnel like this to see that it is clear before entering; wide-beamed boats do use this stretch of the canal. In a longer tunnel, for instance Blisworth on the Grand Union by Stoke Bruerne which is nearly two miles in length, narrow boats enter whether or not they can see an approaching boat, but wide-beamed craft have to make a special arrangement to pass through.

Like the horse we must walk over the top. Leave the towing path up the slope to Muriel Street.   Cross the road bearing right to enter the Half Moon Crescent Housing Co-operative Estate, walk up the path to Maygood Street and continue as far as Barnsbury Road.   On the opposite corner stands White Conduit House, so called because it stood near a white stone conduit which supplied fresh water to Charter-house until 1654 but was removed in 1831.   There has been a small beer-house on this site since 1649 and it later became a "celebrated Cockney place of amusement". In 1754 it was advertised as "having for its fresh attractions a long walk, a circular fish-pond, a number of pleasant shady arbours enclosed with a fence seven feet high, hot loaves and butter, milk direct from the cow, coffee, tea and other liquors, a cricket field, unadulterated cream, and a handsome long room, with copious prospects and airy situation." (30b).   The building is featured on a number of early prints of the canal and Islington Tunnel (see page 24).   However in the 1840s it became a den of vice and debauchery and it was demolished in 1849 to be replaced by the present building.   In the 1870s the aeronaut Charles Green made balloon ascents from the extensive grounds surrounding the tea gardens. A groundsman here was Thomas Lord who later built the cricket ground in Marylebone which bears his name (see page 8).

Continue walking up Dewey Road and cross White Conduit Street, bearing right to Ritchies Street.   We can just see on the right, at the end of White Conduit Street, Chapel Market, a feature of Islington at the weekends.   Ritchies Street leads to Liverpool Road and looking left past the school playground we see the re-furbished Royal Agricultural Hall.   Built 1861–2 and used principally for cattle shows, it also housed such displays as Ashley's Horses, Blondin's Tightrope Act and Bertram Mills Circus and in March, 1870, a group of men, including some Spanish matadors, were prosecuted for promoting bull-fighting there.   In Dickens's Dictionary of London, Charles Dickens Junior recorded in 1877:

"Agricultural Hall, Royal – A building of the railway-station order, close by the Angel at Islington.   The Christmas Cattle show of the Smithfield Club is held here, as are also sundry horse and other shows. The building is now commonly opened during the winter holidays with a variety show in the nature of an old-fashioned fair with menageries, fat ladies, merry-go-rounds, swings, and all the rest of the queer entertain-ments which never seem to lose their popularity.   The Mohawk Minstrels generally occupy the smaller hall with a negro minstrelsey entertainment." (31)

In 1879 an International Pedestrian Match – a six-day foot race – was held there (32a). From 1939 it was used by the Post Office parcels department but since then it has become largely derelict. Various uses were suggested for it, including a sports centre or a Theme Park, with Charles Dickens or Beatrix Potter as the theme, but in 1982 it was bought for £1m from Islington Borough Council and it was reported that a further £7m was to be spent on converting it into the Business Design Centre (32a).   It opened in October, 1986, to provide an exhibition hall, showrooms, a conference centre and three restaurants.

Cross Liverpool Road and walk down Bromfield Street, turning left and right into Berner's Road.   The frontage of the Business Design Centre is reminiscent of the Crystal Palace, the 'Aggie' was built within ten years of the Great Exhibtion in Hyde Park for which the Crystal Palace was constructed.   When the Hall was being refurb-ished a cast-iron walkway, believed to have been part of the Crystal Palace, was discovered among the debris on the second floor.   It is believed that some of the original structure, not re-erected when the Palace was transferred to Sydenham, was used in the Royal Agricultural Hall (32b).   The name from the front of the original

Hall has been erected near the main entrance of the Business Design Centre.

Cross the road by the zebra crossing – the statue of Sir Hugh Myddelton, builder of the New River, is a short distance away on the green to the left – and continue down Charlton Place passing Camden Passage, famed for its antique shops. At the bottom is Colebrooke Row along which the New River once flowed. The New River was built in 1609–13 to bring fresh water to London from springs in Hertfordshire in a forty mile long channel ending at New River Head, next to Sadlers Wells Theatre. Built while Shakespeare was still writing and presenting his plays in London, the New River still supplies London with 38 million gallons of fresh water daily. Look to the left to the last house on the left where Charles Lamb lived with his sister from 1823–1827, it was down his front path that George Dyer, after a visit, walked into the water instead of turning right to retrace the path he had followed on arrival (34). Turn right at the bottom of Colebrooke Row and walk through the little park which is along the old course of the New River.

Leave the garden into Duncan Street and cross the corner of Vincent Terrace where steps lead down to the walk beside the canal. The towing path is actually on the left side, but the slope down which the horse walked from Colebrooke Row is now locked. Alongside the towing path is a row of elegant Georgian mansions in Noel Road, the canalside walk along the right bank has been planted by the London Borough of Islington making this stretch most attractive. Ahead of us is Frog Lane Bridge; climb the steps and cross Danbury Street, to rejoin the towing path by the gate on the left side of the canal.

We come now to City Road Lock and City Road Basin. On the opposite side of the canal is a row of houses, one of which was the lock-keeper's. At the right end of the houses is a sanitary station – now no longer in use – such as is provided throughout the canal system by British Waterways Board. Boat-owners may obtain a key from the Board which fits the locks on all of them and they include facilities for emptying portable toilets. On the left of the canal were stables; it was usual to change the horses three times between Paddington and Limehouse. There is a water point here where boaters may take on fresh water.

City Road Basin, covering four acres, was the principal basin on the canal serving many wharfs and factories. At one time it extended beyond City Road and had several arms off it on the left side. In 1891 there were flour and timber wharfs and wharfs operated by Fellows, Morton and Clayton, the canal carriers, but in the early 1900s a substantial wharfage area was taken over by a pharmaceutical firm, British Drug Houses which had factories on both sides of the basin and they extended over Wharf Road to Wenlock Basin as well. Pickford & Company, and later Carter Patterson, the carrier firm, had property at the City Road end and on the left, near City Road, was one of the five pumping stations of the London Hydraulic Power Company, the only one not by the Thames. The area of the basin has been reduced in stages, first by the closure of the part beyond City Road. In the Evening Standard dated 11 December, 1973, it was reported that "Islington Council has re-affirmed its view that part of the three acre stretch of water in the Canal's City Road Basin will have to be filled in if plans for a big council housing scheme on the banks of the basin are to go ahead." The London Branch of the Inland Waterways Association mounted a rally of boats in the basin to draw attention to the plans and eventually only a small section up to City Road was filled in by the Central Electricity Generating Board in October, 1979. The Islington Boat Club is now based here giving the children of

Islington the opportunity for water sports. All the buildings on the left of the basin have been removed and the flat level area on the corner, which used to be a timber yard, could possibly be used for canal offices. The next bridge is Wharf Road Bridge built about 1830. There is access to the road here, and to the Narrow Boat Pub on Wharf Road. A door just beyond the bridge leads to the pub from the towing path.

City Road Basin 1973
(From author's oil painting)

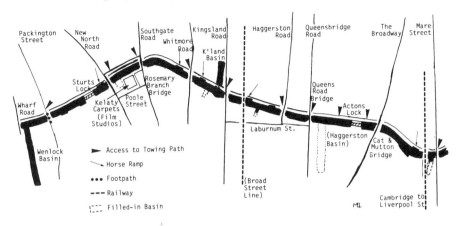

Wharf road marks the boundary between Islington and Hackney, but only as far as the middle of the canal.   From here to Sturts Lock we are walking in Islington – as can be seen from the litter bins – and looking at Hackney across the water.   On the right of the canal a gate from Wharf Road leads to the private moorings in Wenlock Basin;   this basin, built in 1826, occupies about an acre.   On the right, where the boats are now moored, was the site of Wenlock Iron Wharf, and next to it was another B.D.H. drug factory, then the wharfs of Waterlow & Sons, Printers, and finally another drug company, Stafford Allen & Sons.   Basins such as this should provide excellent moorings for pleasure craft but there is often a problem of access as the basins are usually surrounded by private properties.   Close by is Packington Street Bridge, which carries Shepherdess Walk over the canal, and next to it, on the opposite bank, Pilkington Glass had a factory before the second world war.   Between it and Sturts Lock, in 1890, was Henry Rifled Barrel Engineers and Small Arms Ltd., but in the 1930s the factory was taken over as a plywood and wallboard warehouse.   Alongside Sturts Lock, on the towing path side, was another of the pumping stations which back-pumped the water from below Sturts to above City Road Lock (see page 11).   Below the lock on the right bank was once an iron works, there is a horse ramp in the towing path.

Ahead of us is New North Road Bridge, and the building on the right of the bridge marked 'Bridge Works' is now the Oriental Carpet Centre, it is shown on an 1891 map as a drug grinding mill – whatever that might be – and there was a small basin next to it.   Beyond it is a large building with no windows in its right-hand side wall, advertising L Kelaty Ltd., Oriental Carpets Bonded Warehouse.   This used to be the Gainsborough Film Studios.   Built originally as a power station for the Metropolitan Railway, it was taken over in 1919 by a film company, Famous Players – Lasky British Producers Ltd., and converted into two studios where Alfred Hitchcock began his film career.   In 1924 Michael Balcon founded Gainsborough Pictures and bought the Islington Studios;   it was here that Will Hay made many of his films, including "Oh Mr Porter" in 1937, Jessie Matthews made "Climbing High", and Hitchcock made "Lady Vanishes" with Michael Redgrave and Margaret Lockwood in 1939 – the film carries the credit "Made at Islington Studios" though the building has always been in Hackney.   It had two sound stages, one of 92' x 62' on the ground floor and the other of 100' x 46' above it.   During the war it became one of the leading British Film

Gainsborough Pictures

studios, Margaret Lockwood made most of her films here, including "Love Story", "Man in Gray", "Waterloo Road" and "Magic Bow" with Stewart Granger and Phyllis Calvert, and "Fanny by Gaslight" and "Wicked Lady" with James Mason. Here also Carol Reed made "Bank Holiday" and Launder and Gilliat made "Millions Like Us". The entrance in Poole Street still has a small decorative feature over the door, but the building was converted to a distillery when most of the contents were removed and today in the carpet warehouse there is nothing to see of the old Gainsborough Film Studios. It is suggested that beneath the large white L Kelaty Ltd sign on the canal side of the building is the old motif of the lady with the large hat which appeared on all Gainsborough films, but this I have been unable to confirm.

A little further down on the same side is the Crown & Manor Boys Club. There have been boys' clubs here for over a century and in 1926 the Crown Club and the Hoxton Manor Club amalgamated and the purpose-built clubhouse was built for them. Beside the towing path is a CEGB pumping station for cooling the cables under the path. Ahead of us a multicoloured pipe spans the canal. This is a sewer and a proposal to bury it beneath the canal was abandoned when it was discovered that it would cost about £90,000 to do. At the instigation of CHUG — "Canals in Hackney Users' Group" — the pipe has been painted. However the specification was that it should be painted like a rainbow over the canal; something went wrong and the colours of the rainbow were applied in seven blocks — red, orange, yellow, green, blue, indigo and violet — instead of as arcs across the water. It is, nevertheless, a decorative feature alongside Rosemary Branch Bridge. There has been a Rosemary Branch Tavern in this area for over a century and a public house of that name is still in Shepperton Road, opposite the access gate from the towing path here.

Whitmore Bridge, one of the bridges built when the canal was under construction in about 1820, leads to De Beauvoir Road, Crescent and Square, formerly de Beauvoir Town. Sir George Whitmore, who became Lord Mayor of London, built his residence "on a scale of great magnificence" in the early part of the seventeenth century to the north of where the canal is now; this was later purchased by Richard de Beauvoir, a Guernsey gentleman, who lived there in great style. The house subsequently acquired a moat with draw-bridges leading to beautiful gardens, but in the nineteenth century the building became dilapidated and after being used for a time as a private lunatic asylum, it was demolished in about 1850. The horse ramp in the towing path along here is in a very good state of repair and it is easy to see the slope up which horses could be led after they had fallen into the canal. There was a small basin, now filled in, on the opposite bank.

Further along, the towing path rises over the entrance to another basin, Kingsland Basin, built in 1830 and served timber and stone wharfs, a large manure wharf and a refuse wharf. There used to be an arm off it on the right adjacent to the towing path but it has been filled in and built over. The basin is now administered by CHUG (see above) and is a mooring for privately owned pleasure craft. Close by is Kingsland Road Bridge. This area was once the southern extremity of the Forest of Middlesex which extended from Houndsditch in the south to Enfield Chace in the north, and it was here that royalty used to hunt, it is suggested that the name Kingsland was derived from this. In his Diary entry for 12 May, 1667, Samuel Pepys wrote: "Walked over the fields to Kingsland, and back again; a walk, I think, I have not taken these twenty years; but puts me in mind of my boy's time when I boarded at Kingsland, and used to shoot with my bow and arrows in these fields." Kingsland Road is now the A10 to Hertford and Cambridge and it can be seen, beneath the bridge, how the road has been widened with newer brickwork on either side of the old. Immediately beyond the bridge is a railway bridge which, until recently, carried the North London line from Richmond into Broad Street Station, with a horse ramp beneath it.

A large brick wall now dominates the canal on its right side where the Gas, Light & Coke Co.Ltd. had its gas works in Laburnham Street, with its basin, where coal was delivered by barge, at its eastern end; this has been shortened and is now used by the Laburnham Street School. On the wall by the basin is a (faded) notice advertising CHUG. The Canals in Hackney Users' Group aims to improve the canals in the Borough for all who use them — boaters, anglers, swimmers, towing-path walkers, cyclists, and so on — and improvements are evident. There is another excellent horse ramp in the towing path. Opposite the school, alongside the towing path on the left, are some magnificent mosaics undertaken by Free Form Arts Trust in collaboration with the school staff and children and other local groups. These extend on to the next bridge, Haggerston Bridge, where the school is identified, and beyond it along the wall. There seems to be a representation of some of the school children and at the end is a marvellous narrow boat passing under a bridge. On Haggerston bridge the iron guards to protect the stonework have been deeply grooved by ropes towing barges.

On the other side of Queen's Road Bridge — over which runs Queensbridge Road — on the right is a section of piling which was the entrance to the immense Haggerston Basin which extended far beyond Whiston Street to the gas works. It is now filled in, the part south of Whiston Street for a recreation ground, and new building is taking place on the section nearer the canal. Notice how the housing estate bordering the canal on the towing path side has been opened up to the water with railings in place of walls. We see this improvement to the environment along the canal in several places.

The next lock is Actons Lock — named after a Mr Joe Acton through whose land the canal was dug. Beyond it is Cat & Mutton Bridge, so called because the road was once named Mutton Lane on which stood the Cat & Mutton public house. The inn, we are told (35), carried two sign boards with the lines:

> "Pray, Puss, do not tare,
> Because the Mutton is so rare."

> "Pray, Puss, do not claw,
> Because the Mutton is so raw."

Mutton Lane is now Goldsmiths Row south of the bridge and Broadway Market north of it. The Sir Walter Scott which overlooks the canal here is not the site of the Cat & Mutton; a pub of that name stands at the far end of The Broadway.

Derelict Warehouse advertising for staff, below Actons Lock

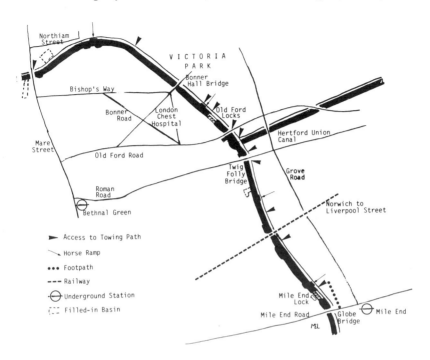

Continue under the bridge and notice, on the right of the canal a large derelict warehouse – 'J. S. DARV. . . .' – which looks as if there has been a fire in it; on the wall half way along is a neat wooden notice "Lyfada Ltd, Manufacturers of Ladies Coats : Suits : Jackets. Staff Wanted. Apply ground floor (Wharf Place)". Developers seem now to be moving in.   On the corner beyond it is a group of massive gas holders built for the Gas, Light & Coke Co. Ltd.; its wharfs where coal was unloaded from barges lay alongside the canal.   There is another CEGB pumping station alongside the towing path here.   Ahead of us the Liverpool Street to Cambridge line crosses high over the canal with Cambridge Heath Bridge beyond it.   Between the two, on the other side of the water is an oblique brick arch which was the entrance to a basin which served a timber yard.   The rubble tipped into the old arm makes a very unattractive view.   Mare Street crosses the canal here.

On the other side of the bridge the canal widens on the right at the site of an old wharf and a short distance along on the left, beside the towing path, is the blocked-up entrance to a basin which used to serve a stone and marble works and a timber wharf; some sources refer to it as Gerver's Basin, others as North Street or Northiam Basin. The road passing it was North Street and is now Northiam Street.   The entrance is closed with unsightly sheets of corrugated iron and it is possible to discern where the towing path crossed it.   The canal starts a broad sweep to the right and as we round the bend, passing another horse ramp in the towing path, we experience a contrasting change of scenery.

61

Bonner Hall Bridge, Victoria Park

The Regent's Canal forms the south-west boundary of Victoria Park, 217 acres laid out in 1842–45 by James Pennethorne at a cost of £50,000. Pennethorne was the assistant to John Nash who handed over to him his entire practice in 1834 shortly before he died. This is London's oldest municipal park. The housing estate on the right, facing the park, has recently been opened up to the canal with brightly painted railings and a picnic area. The canal was dug through land previously known as 'Bishop Bonner's Fields' in which once stood the residence of Bishop Bonner during the reign of King Henry VIII. The unpopularity of the Bishop may be gauged from allusions to him such as "Bishop Bonner, the sworn enemy of Protestants . . ." (36a)₁) and ". . .the court in which the awful Bonner exercised his tyrannical and cruel sway . . ." (36b). The bridge across the canal was the main entrance to the Park and is called Bonner Hall Bridge — the elegant brick columns, up on the right of the bridge, used to carry the gates. Close by is Bishop's Way and Bonner Road and the site of the Bishop's mansion is thought to have been about here, near where the London Chest Hospital, built in 1851, now stands. There are public toilets in the park near the road from Bonner Hall Bridge and there is access to the park nearer the lock, opposite a horse ramp.

Old Ford Lock — Regent's (not to be confused with Old Ford Locks — Lee, which are on the Lee Navigation at the other end of Old Ford Road, about a mile and a half away) used to be known by boatmen as Longford Lock (27), and here stood another of the back-pumping stations (see page 11) and stables for a change of horses. At the foot of the locks on the right, beside Old Ford Road bridge, stands the Royal Cricketers public house; there is access to the road from the towing path. Just beyond the bridge on the right is a small basin, Bridge Wharf, on which was a storage warehouse, owned by the Northern Metropolitan Tramway Co.Ltd. The Lower East Side Restaurant on Old Ford Road is there now and the barge in the basin provides a reception area for lunches and meetings.

Ahead of us the towing path rises over an entrance suggesting another basin on the left. This is the Hertford Union Canal, or Duckett's Canal, linking the Regent's Canal with the River Lee Navigation. Opened in 1830 by Sir George Duckett, it is one and a quarter miles long and has three locks on it near the far end. This provided a short cut for traffic from the Lee wishing to travel up the Regent's Canal and the Grand Junction Canal to the Midlands; previously it would have had to continue down the Lee and the Limehouse Cut, lock into the Thames through the Limehouse Barge Lock and return through the Regent's Canal Ship Lock, and work up the four locks on the Regent's Canal below Old Ford Lock to reach this point. As canals were traditionally known as 'the cut' one wonders if this might have been the origin of the phrase 'a short cut'. Notice the widening of the canal opposite the entrance to Ducketts to allow narrow boats to turn when entering or leaving the branch canal.

Between this winding hole and the next bridge there used to be a firm of barge builders with its wharfs on the canal. Roman Road crosses the canal by Twig Folly Bridge, and beyond this, on the right, is the large canopy of a warehouse overhanging the water. This is Suttons Timber Wharf, which now seems to contain more timber products – paper and packing materials – than timber. The railway line crossing the canal is the Liverpool Street to Norwich Line and beyond it are some warehouses on the opposite bank, some of them with large double-doors which open on to their wharfs beside the water. All along beside the towing path will be seen evidence of the improvements made by the Local Authority in opening up the canal to the community and providing open spaces and seats overlooking the water. We come now to Mile End Lock with its attractive lockhouse on the right. There is a gate from the towing path here which gives access to Mile End Road which crosses the next bridge – Globe Bridge.

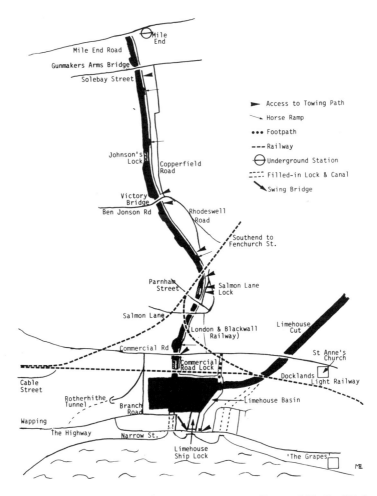

Mile End Road is the A11 from east London into Essex; Mile End Tube Station is a short distance along to the left and Queen Mary College, University of London, is to the right. Across the canal a little further along is Gunmaker's Arms Bridge which now carries Solebay Street. A new housing development on the right on either side of the bridge has provided an attractive frontage overlooking the canal. F. Allen & Sons, confectionery manufacturers, had several works along the canal here and by Devon Wharf, a short distance below the bridge, was its cocoa and chocolate works — near the Ocean Pirate Club. On the left is Falcon Works; once a shirt and collar works, it now makes blouses and dresses. The series of buildings from here to the next bridge housed several factories on Copperfield Road.

On the central island of Johnson's Lock, between the locks — the further one has now been converted to a weir — is a post carrying a rack and pinion which used to operate the paddle which controlled the flow between the two locks (see page 20). There was once such a paddle on every lock on the Regent's Canal but they have all been removed except this one and the one at Hampstead Road Top Lock. Alongside the lock is the abandoned factory of Watford Chemical Co, and next to it was a pharmaceutical manufactory. Below the lock was another of Allen's confectionery works and a lime-juice factory, with a Dr Barnado's School happily situated between them. The school was opened in 1877 and in 1896 extended into the lime-juice factory, but the school closed in 1908. The property is now owned by the Ragged School Museum Trust which is seeking to restore and preserve the old buildings. The confectionery factory is now used by a packing and distributing firm. On the right-hand bank of the canal, between the lock and the next bridge, were the extensive wharfs of the gas works, along which ran a coal tramway.

The bridge ahead of us is Victory Bridge, which carries Ben Jonson Road over the canal. It is strange that the lock, so close to this road, has a different spelling from it. Ben Jonson Road joins Rhodeswell Road which swings round to border the canal on the left side. At its end, just before the railway bridge and standing beside the towing path, is a brick stack which looks as if the factory it served has been removed. In fact it is the ventilation shaft of a sewer. The railway is the Fenchurch Street to Southend line. Salmon Lane lock has its lock cottage on the left and there is a path behind it giving access to Parnham Road, Salmon Lane and Commercial Road. Crossing the canal just beyond it is the now disued branch railway line from Stratford and Bow to the Isle of Dogs and Millwall Docks. Beside the towing path along here was the Regent's Canal Works of the Gospel Oak Iron Company, occupying the triangle of land between the railway and Commercial Road. Before reaching the bridge, notice on the left in the bank alongside the towing path a rusted iron control valve and inspection cover; this used to operate the back-pumping along the towing path from the Thames to above Mile End Lock.

Preserved Central Paddle Gear Johnsons Lock

65

There are two arches over the canal through Commercial Road Bridge leading to Commercial Road Lock; as the right hand lock has been converted into a weir, craft must take the left arch. Walk under the Bridge; attached to it, over the lock, is a 36-inch iron pipe. This is part of the back-pumping system carrying water, drawn from the Thames on the far side of Limehouse Basin, to reach the towing path (see page 11). On the left there is an opening through the building leading to steps up to Commercial Road, the A13 road to East Ham and Barking.

The entry to Limehouse Basin is under an arch of the elegant 1838 viaduct built to carry the London and Blackwall Railway 3½ miles from the Minories to Blackwall Docks. The railway was initially intended only for passengers to take them to ships in the Docks or to steamers to resorts in the estuary (37). When it opened on 4 July, 1840, the carriages were drawn by cables – Cable Street lies alongside the line between the Minories and Limehouse Basin – but in 1848 locomotives were introduced; an iron roof was erected over the Limehouse Viaduct to prevent sparks from the engines setting fire to the sailing ships or their cargoes of timber in the Docks. The line closed in 1926 and the rails were finally removed in 1962. New tracks have now been laid as part of the Docklands Light Railway, which is expected to open for passengers in July 1987 from Tower Gateway to Island Gardens on the Isle of Dogs, close to the entrance to the Greenwich foot tunnel. An extension westwards to Bank underground station is planned.

Commercial Road lock is the twelfth lock from Hampstead Road and leads directly into Limehouse Basin – which used to be called Regent's Canal Dock when it was busy. The whole of this area is due for development; British Waterways Board invited several organisations to submit schemes and on 4 February, 1982, announced that it had chosen a seventy million pounds scheme to provide 600 housing units, 50,000 sq. ft. of hypermarket, 66,000 sq.ft. of shops, 36,000 sq.ft. of offices, two public houses, restaurants, and a marina and workshop complex (38). A public inquiry was held in 1983 and despite the recommendation by the Government appointed inspectors that planning permission should be refused, approval was given. The Limehouse Development Group, formed by local people in 1979, had prepared an alternative scheme and in June 1986 launched a 'Limehouse Petition'.

As development proceeds it will be difficult to see the interesting historical features around the basin; I shall describe them as they appear at the beginning of 1987. Look across the basin slightly to the right; two large buoys lie in the water and behind them is some black iron piling with a wall projecting into the basin on its right. This was the entrance to the barge lock, the first lock to the Thames which is now covered over. In fact the lock chamber is intact with a roof over it and the single electric lamp over the water lying in the bottom of the chamber makes it very eerie. The roof serves as a car park for the offices. The building on the right of this old lock was the pumping station which sent the water from the Thames up the towing path.

Ahead of us, and slightly to the left, is the entrance to the Ship Lock, which is 350 feet long, 60 feet wide, and has a depth of 26 feet below high water. The water level in the Basin is semi-tidal; the Limehouse Cut communicates with the tidal River Lee through Bow Locks and these locks are opened three hours before high tide and closed three hours after it. This semi-tidal length is therefore maintained at a minimum depth but rises and falls during the six hours around full tide. Commercial Road Locks, together with Old Ford Locks – Lee, are the junctions of the maintained level of the canals with the semi-tidal stretch of water from Limehouse basin, up Limehouse Cut and up the lower Lee Navigation.

It was possible to walk round the left side of the basin, over a footbridge, and along the east side of the ship lock to Narrow Street, but at the moment this route is fenced off. The alternative is to climb the steps on the right of the canal locks into Commercial Road, walk to the left and take the first turning on the left which leads towards the mouth of Rotherhithe Tunnel. Bear left down Branch Road and turn left into The Highway. A short distance along, on the left, is the old back-pumping station and next to it the site of the disused barge Lock. Follow the road round to the right and turn left into Narrow Street which crosses the ship lock over a swing bridge. The lock house and control cabin are on the right. At the moment this is a British Waterways Board office concerned with the Regent's Canal but a proposal to site a pub and restaurant at the lock entrance means that the Board will have to find new accommodation for its staff; land cleared at City Road Basin might be a good site.

Look across the ship lock into Limehouse Basin. Ahead, slightly to the right, is the tower of St Anne, Limehouse, a Hawksmoor church built in 1712 (see page 23). To the left of it is a more modern church with a statue on it; this is the R.C. Church of Our Lady Immaculate, Limehouse, built in 1934. In line with the lock, to the left of the Catholic Church, is a dark brick tower, an accumulator tower of 1852. The docks in London began introducing hydraulic power to operate their cranes, hoists and derricks in 1852; small pumping stations were built to force water to the machinery and the pressurised water was stored in accumulator towers. The Regent's Canal Dock pumping station stood on the left of the tower and the remnants of the chimney can still be seen attached behind the tower. This was probably the first hydraulic pumping station in the country. The many hydraulic power networks, each serving a small amount of equipment, proved uneconomical and this led, in 1871, to the foundation of the London Hydraulic Power Company (see page 11).

Limehouse Basin from Ship Lock
Looking North on the skyline, left to right are the Accumulator Tower,
Church of St. Mary Immaculate & Church of St. Anne.

Before exploring Limehouse basin itself it is interesting to walk up Narrow Street eastwards from the swing bridge; the bridge over the Limehouse Barge Lock is a short distance along. The River Lee flows into the Thames by Bow Creek, a two-mile estuary joining the Thames downstream of the Isle of Dogs, and navigable only at high tide. Following the River Lea Act of 1766 — which called for new locks and straightening of the river to improve navigation — the Limehouse Cut was dug from the Lee at Bow, across the neck of the Isle of Dogs, to the Limehouse Barge Lock into the Thames at Limehouse. The barge lock was on an awkward angle and needed winches to open the gates and though the Regent's Canal Ship Lock was built along-side it there was no communication between the two. In 1967 the barge lock was in urgent need of repair but its closure would have seriously disrupted River Lee traffic. Instead a link between Limehouse Cut and Regent's Canal Dock, fifty feet wide, seven feet deep, and two hundred feet long, was built at a cost of £120,000 and the barge lock closed on 1 April 1968 — one of the winches is preserved at Hampstead Road Top Lock (see page 44). The old lock is heavily overgrown and the lockhouse and the bridges under Narrow Street and Northey Street have been bricked up; the entrance from the River Thames is on our right.

Further along the road some of the houses built in 1734 still remain and on the right, on the bank of the Thames, is The Grapes, which featured in Charles Dicken's "Our Mutual Friend" as the 'Six Jolly Fellowship Porters'. The present building replaced the earlier one destroyed by fire in the nineteenth century. Another prominent 19th Century pub, on the left, is The House they left Behind. Residents in this area include the Rt Hon David Owen, leader of the SDP; Ian McKellan, the actor; Steven Berkoff, the writer and director; David Lean, the film director; Jeremy Wallington, founder of Limehouse Studios, and Lady Raynes.

Return to the swing bridge; over the ship lock west of here is the Rotherhithe tunnel and beyond it is Wapping where the newspaper offices of the Times and Sunday Times, the Sun and News of the World opened recently. Go down the steps on the right to walk along beside the ship lock and the basin. On the right, just inside the basin, stood the customs office; on this south east quay were a six-ton and two two-ton cranes. The footbridge ahead of us crosses the new entrance to Limehouse Cut. There were four jetties projecting into the water, two from the west quay on the far side of the basin and two on the north quay, east of the entrance to the Regent's Canal; one of these remains. The Regent's Canal Dock ceased to be a commercial dock in 1969 and its name was changed to Limehouse Basin; the cranes were later removed and some of them were taken to Gloucester Dock by the British Waterways Board.

A gate under the Docklands Light Railway leads to Commercial Road; the accummulator tower and old pumping station are on the left. St Anne's Church is usually locked but it is well worth arranging a visit. From July 1987 it will be possible to catch a train from Limehouse station on the Docklands Light Railway — turn left along Commercial Road — but until then the nearest tube is Mile End.

REFERENCES

1. Nicholson's Guide to the Waterways, 4: North East. P.67 British Waterways Board, 1972

2. Canals of Eastern England by John Boyes and Ronald Russell; David & Charles, 1977 p.172

3. A Guide to the Roman Remains in Britain by Roger J.A. Wilson; Constable, London, 1975 p.155

4. Roman Britain by John Wacher; Dent, London, 1978 p.131

5. Navigation of the River Lee – 1190–1790 by J.G.L. Burnby and M. Parker; Edmonton Hundred Historical Society – Occasional Paper (New Series) No. 36, 1978

6. Canal Age by Charles Hadfield; Pan Books, 1968 a) p.3; b) p.138; c) p.120

7. Old and New London, Vol.5, by Edward Walford; Cassell, Petter & Galpin, 1873–1878, a) p.302; b) p.256; c) p.352; d) p.298

8. A Short History of Nuffield Lodge, Regent's Park by Penelope Hunting; Nuffield Foundation, 1974

9. London's Canal by Herbert Spencer; Lund Humphries, London, 1976

10. Public Record Office; Reports and letters written by John Nash to the Commissioners of His Majesty's Woods, Forests & Land Revenues. a) CRES 2/1736; b) LRRO 60/751; c) copy seen at Marylebone Library.

11. Tour of the Grand Junction Canal by John Hassell; Printed for J. Hassell, 1819; p.6

12. Gentleman's Magazine and Historical Chronicle; a) Vol. 89 Pt ii, August 1819, p.105; b) Vol. 82 Pt i, Suppt. 1812, p.650; c) Vol.82 Pt ii, October 1812, p.388

13. Old and New London, Vol.5. by Edward Walford; Cassell, Petter & Galpin, 1873–1878, p.369

14. Story of Agar Town by Revd. R. Couzens Morrell, 1935

15. London's Waterways by Martyn Denney; Batsford, London, 1977.

16. Improved Modes of Constructing Locks and Sluices of Canals by William Congreve; Patent No. 3670, 1813.

17. The Times, 2 August, 1820; British Library Newspaper Library

18. The Living Thames by John Doxat, Hutchinson Benham, London, 1977

19. Pipe Dreams by Michael Essex-Lopresti; BWB Waterways News, No.103, September 1980, p.10

20. Harpers Monthly Magazine, Vol. LXX, No. 420, May 1885 pp.857–876. London Borough of Camden Local History Department: Heal Collection

21. Canals and their Architecture by Robert Harris; Hugh Evelyn, 1869, p.120

22. Illustrated London News; Saturday 10 October,1874. Heal Collection, Camden Local History Department.

23. London's Canal – Its Past, Present and Future; 1969, London Canals Consultative Committee

24. The Darbys and the Ironbridge Gorge by Brian Bracegirdle and Patricia H Miles; David & Charles, 1974

25. Canal Walks in London by Marie Rodda; London Visitor & Convention Bureau, 1985

26. Historical Account of the Navigable Rivers, Canals and Railways throughout Britain by Joseph Priestley; London, 1831

27. The Amateur Boatwoman by Eily Gayford; David & Charles, 1973

28. The Lady's Newspaper; No.211, Saturday, January 11, 1851, p.21

29. Speculum Britanniae – the first part. A description of Middlesex. By John Norden; 1593. p.15

30. Old and New London, Vol. 2 by Walter Thornbury; Cassell, Petter & Galpin, 1873–1978, a) p.278; b) p.279

31. Dickens's Dictionary of London by Charles Dickens; London – MacMillan & Co., 1877

32. The Times, a) Thursday 29 July, 1982; b) Friday 30 August, 1985

33. The Daily Telegraph; a series of articles on the Canals in London, 22–29 June, 1925

34. Exploring the New River by Michael Essex-Lopresti; Brewin Books, 1986, p.18

35. Old and New London, Vol.5 by Edward Walford; Cassell, Petter & Galpin, 1873–1878, p.507

36. The Gentleman's Magazine and Historical Chronicle a) Vol.76, Pt ii, July 1806, p.597; b) Vol. 98, pt ii, December 1828, p.501

37. A Journey through History – a set of leaflets published by Docklands Light Railway Limited

38. Waterways News, No.118, March 1982, p.1; Published by British Waterways Board.

Further Reading

Grand Junction Canal by Alan H Faulkner, David & Charles, 1972

On the Canal by John Hollingshead, 1973; reprinted from 'Household Words' by British Waterways Board

London's Canal by Herbert Spencer; Lund Humphries, London, 1976

London's Waterway Guide by Chris Cove-Smith; Imray, Laurie, Norrie & Wilson, 1977

London's Waterways by Martyn Denney; B.T. Batsford, Ltd., 1977

Back Door Britain by Anthony Burton; Andre Deutsch, 1977

Discovering London's Canals by Derek Pratt; Shire Publications, 1977

Through London by Canal, 1977. Extracts from Harpers New Monthly Magazine 1885, published by British Waterways Board

Industrial Archaeology Walks in London by David G. Thomas, a series of leaflets published by Camden History Society and Greater London Industrial Archaeology Society

Kings Cross Cut by Bob Gilbert. Published by the Kings Cross Canal Project in conjunction with the Thornhill Neighbourhood Centre; July 1985

A Short History of the Regent's Canal, published by the British Waterways Board, 1986

Wild Flowers of the Waterways and Marshes by E.A. Ellis, 1973; Jarrold & Sons, Norwich

Birds of the Inland Waters and Marshes by Reg Jones, 1978; Jarrold & Sons, Norwich

Also

Barging Through London, a silent film in the "Wonderful London" series, by Harry B. Parkinson, 1924. The same shots filmed again by John Huntley and Michael Essex-Lopresti in 1979, intercut with the original. Barging through London Again, 16mm, silent, available from the author.

Addresses

Inland Waterways Association, 114 Regent's Park Road, London NW1 8UQ
(01 586 2510 & 2556)

Jason's Trip, Barge Tab, 66 Blomfield Road, London W9
(01 286 3428)

Jenny Wren Canal Cruises, 250 Camden High Street, London NW1
(01 485 4433)

London Canals Project Officer, BWB Canal Office, Delamere Terrace, W2 6ND
(01 289 9897)

London Waterbus Co., Camden Lock, London NW1 8AF
(01 482 2550)

Regent's Canal Information Centre, 280 Camden High Street, London NW1 7BX
(01 482 0523)

ILLUSTRATIONS

MAPS

INDEX

Acton's Lock 11,59
Agar, William 5, 8, 22, 30, 49
Agar Town 3, 29, 30, 31, 49

Battlebridge 2, 8, 20, 22, 52
British Waterways Board 16, 17, 18, 19, 20, 34, 42, 50, 66, 68

CEGB cables 11, 19, 20, 35, 43, 58
Camden 19, 21, 23, 29, 34, 39, 47, 49, 50, 51, 52
Camden Lock Centre 44
City Road Basin 9, 12, 15, 55
City Road Lock 11, 55, 57
Commercial Road Locks 11, 66
Congreve, Colonel William 7, 9
Cumberland Basin 2, 7, 39, 40, 41

Docklands Light Railway 66, 68

Elmes, James 3, 38
Euston Station 3, 15, 29, 40, 43
Explosives Act−1874 15

Gainsborough Film Studios 57, 58
Gas works 50, 51, 59, 61, 65
Grand Junction Canal 2, 4, 8, 9, 11, 12, 16, 22, 34, 63
Grand Union Canal 12, 14, 16, 19, 20, 34, 63
Great Centra Railway 36
Great Northern Railway 15, 49, 50, 51
Guided Walks along the Regent's Canal 21

Hackney 17, 29, 22, 57, 58
Hampstead Road Lock 7, 19, 20, 21, 33, 44, 45, 65
Hawksmoor, Nicholas 23, 67
Hawley lock 45
Hertford Union Canal 12, 19, 20, 35, 63
Homer, Thomas 4, 5, 6, 8
Horse ramps 15, 19, 39, 42, 43, 49, 52, 57, 59, 62
Horsfall, William 8, 17, 52

Inland Waterways Association 17, 19, 21, 55
Islington 2, 4, 17, 19, 21, 51, 52, 55, 57
Islington tunnel 8, 9, 14, 16, 19, 24, 26, 33, 35, 53
Islington tunnel tug 14, 27, 53

Jason's Trip 21, 34, 39, 43
Jenny Wren 21, 39, 43, 45
Johnsons Lock 20, 64

Kentish Town Lock 11, 45
Kings Cross 2, 3, 15, 52
Kings Cross station 3, 15, 29, 50, 51
Kingsland Basin 20, 59

Legging 14, 26, 35, 53
Limehouse 2, 4, 8, 9, 11, 17, 23, 25, 33, 44, 67

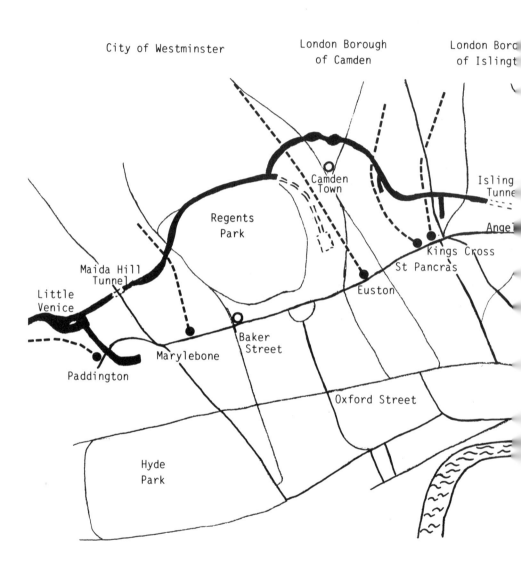

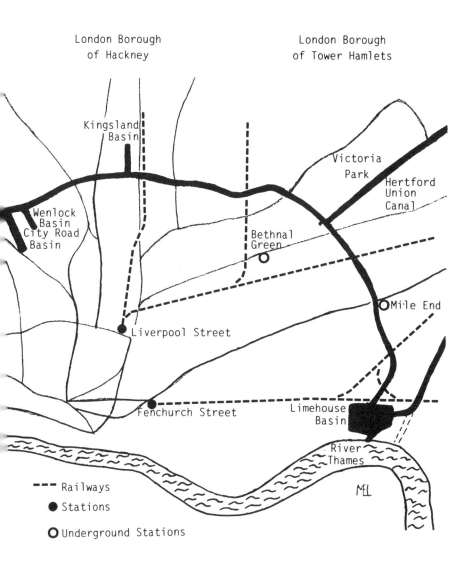

London Borough
of Hackney

London Borough
of Tower Hamlets

Kingsland
Basin

Victoria
Park

Hertford
Union
Canal

Wenlock
Basin
City Road
Basin

Bethnal
Green

Mile End

Liverpool Street

Fenchurch Street

Limehouse
Basin

River
Thames

MEL

--- Railways

● Stations

O Underground Stations

NOTES

EXPLORING THE NEW RIVER

The New River is neither new nor a river but a four hundred year old canal winding through Hertfordshire and Middlesex and still supplying London with over 38 million gallons of water per day. Dr. Essex-Lopresti, a canal enthusiast and authority, has produced a book which combines the history of this little known waterway with detailed maps and routes permitting all those interested in old canals and industrial archaeology to make their own exploration of The New River.

Many maps and illustrations.

Dr. Essex-Lopresti has owned a canal boat since 1972 and while cruising with his wife, they have taken the opportunity of exploring the countryside and visiting places of interest alongside the waterway. On one such excursion they discovered the New River and on seeking information on it were disappointed to find no book available.

The history of inland waterways in Britain is an absorbing study and when asked by the Inland Waterways Association in 1976 to institute guided walks along the Regent's Canal in London, he happily undertook the necessary research and the monthly walks are now in their tenth year. This led to requests for lectures to the London and other branches of the I.W.A., first on the Regent's Canal, and subsequently on other waterways, including the New River. He now lectures frequently to many audiences, mainly in the areas through which the New River runs.

The study of the New River during the past twelve years has revealed a wealth of material gathered from a surprising number of sources including reference libraries, archives and literature, all of which had to be consulted on a part-time basis when time permitted.

Other interests of Dr. Essex-Lopresti include bird-watching – a hobby sparked off by seeing birds on the canals – and theatre.

£4.80 (Net U.K. only)   ISBN 0 947731 12 1

KAF Brewin Books Studley, Warks.

NOTES